JEFFREY W. AUBUCHON

Big Island Santa

92252 PRESS

First published by 92252 Press 2024

Copyright © 2024 by Jeffrey W. Aubuchon

All rights reserved. No part of this publication may be reproduced, stored or transmitted in any form or by any means, electronic, mechanical, photocopying, recording, scanning, or otherwise without written permission from the publisher. It is illegal to copy this book, post it to a website, or distribute it by any other means without permission.

Jeffrey W. Aubuchon has no responsibility for the persistence or accuracy of URLs for external or third-party Internet Websites referred to in this publication and does not guarantee that any content on such Websites is, or will remain, accurate or appropriate.

Designations used by companies to distinguish their products are often claimed as trademarks. All brand names and product names used in this book and on its cover are trade names, service marks, trademarks and registered trademarks of their respective owners. The publishers and the book are not associated with any product or vendor mentioned in this book. None of the companies referenced within the book have endorsed the book.

First edition

ISBN: 978-1-73-405929-8

*This book was professionally typeset on Reedsy.
Find out more at reedsy.com*

*To my mom—who always makes Christmas special.
And to the memory of my grandmothers,
Mémère Legere and Mémère Aubuchon,
who trained my mother and sister in the festive arts.
Thankfully, ma Tante Loretta still ties us to that old world.*

*As Father Christmas—Clark W. Griswold—said in 1989,
"Nobody's walking out on this fun,
old-fashioned, family Christmas."*

"Christmas was on its way. Lovely, glorious, beautiful Christmas, upon which the entire kid-year revolved."

—A Christmas Story (1983)

Prologue: Here Comes Santa Claus

Christmas has us bow to tradition. We use Gram's recipe–and her recipe only–for the eggnog with fortifying spirits and we unearth Mom's gravy boat from the pantry for the special meals. We gather to watch Father Christmas himself, Chevy Chase, on the television and we laugh because Dad laughs at the same jokes year after year. Sometimes, however, our holiday traditions are disrupted, maybe for a sick relative or because of a long-term relocation. Perhaps we rely on our memories more when we are away than when we are closer to home.

In 2019 I relocated to Southern California and, while spending Christmas Day in Joshua Tree National Park hardly represented a typical celebration for this native New Englander, my husband and I cobbled together enough Christmas artifacts to achieve a verisimilitude of home in the desert. I shared another experience years earlier as a Peace Corps Volunteer when I gathered with friends and sang Christmas carols on what was, to our neighbors, just another weeknight in Morocco.

I failed to cultivate Christmas when we moved from SoCal to the Big Island of Hawaii in 2022. I searched for Christmas that year like mapless Magi and I could not find it "in the land where palm trees sway," as Bing sang. In my holiday humbug, I struggled to understand the surprising eruption of emotions I experienced while living some 5,000 miles from New England. My melancholy differed from homesickness; I felt like an outsider in Hawaii or a citizen unwelcome in his own country. Part of *Big Island Santa*, especially the last section, explains how I tried to avoid a "blue" Christmas.

This book is for those of you who have also tried to capture Christmas while being far away from home, or even in the face of changing circumstances nearby. Much like my previous feel-good title, *Put Your Toe in the Pacific*, please share and gift this book. Send it to the soldier, seaman, airman, or the Corpsmen (Marines and Peace) who are serving abroad this year. Send it to the kid or the cousin who has moved far away this holiday. The reading is light, laughable, and thinly-sliced for easy digestion with a glass of mulled wine after Sunday dinner.

Mémère's stockings—my favorite things at Christmas

In our family, my mother safeguards the festive arts she learned from true masters: her mother Noella (Mémère Legere) and mother-in-law Jeannette (Mémère Aubuchon). Although we are grown, Mom still hangs our stockings—knitted by Mémère Aubuchon—with care and cooks all our favorite holiday foods: Mémère Legere's seafood chowder, green bean casserole, ham, twice-baked potatoes, sugared carrots, and the list goes blessedly on and on. What are those prized memories for you? I invite you throughout the book to reflect not on my memories, but those memories my words might spark in you. I included twenty-five questions at the end of the book and presented the list as a holiday game for either self-reflection or party entertainment.

At the conclusion of his 1843 *A Christmas Carol*, Dickens wrote of Scrooge: "It was always said of him that he knew how to keep Christmas well, if any man alive possessed the knowledge. May that be truly said of us, and all of us!" Dickens left us a perennial question, usually probed through both television and Christmas sermons: How do we keep and celebrate Christmas today? The question implies that we should, like Scrooge and Charlie Brown, reject commercialization and kindle the traditions of the heart, even though Scrooge gave the Cratchits a really good Christmas from his purse. The Bible says that Jesus entered the world poor and we should embrace that poverty with a thankful heart, conveniently overlooking the tradition that three wealthy kings gave him luxe gifts of gold and perfume. Perhaps the Christmas message strikes a constant tension between plutocratic wise men and charity to homeless refugees like Jesus, Mary, and Joseph. I conclude the book by sharing my own struggle to make merry and make money during that first Christmas in Hawaii.

Like Dickens', the book in your hands is a mercantile memoir of Christmases past and especially a book about my grandparents. In his recent eulogy to my grandfather, who rejoined my grandmother after twenty years apart, my cousin Tom reflected on the abundance with which my grandparents blessed their family, heralding a wonderful call to the Christmas generosity shared by the Aubuchons even in the heat of that August funeral. Similarly, this story points to the oft-told admonition to find Christmas in the face of Father Commerce, a lesson that began when Joseph failed to reserve a room at the original holiday inn.

As in the tale of the Bethlehem-bound couple, the story of Big Island Santa offers a bit more of a travelogue than other holiday classics. Like the Frenchman Alexis de Tocqueville traveling in the United States some 200 years ago, perhaps I am something of a French Canadian outsider peering into island life—and I don't mean Prince Edward Island. In drawing those Christmas comparisons between Hawaii and New England, I try to get at the enchantment of Christmas rather than its history. Furthermore, I wonder how we share Christmas in this new COVID world where Santa covers his beard with a surgical mask? Or how do we celebrate a climate-conscious Christmas as the North Pole melts? Lastly, please note that like Santa's story, mine only *starts* as non-fiction.

I

Mostly Americana

"A good conscience is a continual Christmas."
—Benjamin Franklin

While living overseas in Hawaii, I rediscovered some
of my favorite Christmas things.

Beginning to Look Like

My Christmas story comes not from Dickens in old England but from the stories of my father and grandfathers in New England. Before inflatable lawn decorations trended, the Union Products Company of Leominster, Massachusetts manufactured plastic injection-molded holiday characters to accent twinkling house lights. As a kid, Christmas meant placing those precious decorations on the brown November lawn to herald the coming festivities. My grandfather managed production at Union Products and oversaw the roll out of not only Santas and snowmen, but also perennially-pink plastic flamingos.

My grandfather, Pépère Aubuchon, spent all of his 92 years abundantly helping and giving to others. In my youth, he gave us an oversized plastic Santa face, which Dad always hung on the garage to greet arriving visitors, along with a four-foot-tall plastic Santa reading his list. With just two Santas, we offered our neighbors a modestly-illuminated display compared to others who filled their yard with dressed snowmen, posed reindeer, stiff nutcrackers, and the holy plastic family. From then until now, my mother's seasonal mantra remains, "the yard must look classy, not tacky."

Grandparents' abundance, with cousin Brian, c. 1984

In late November 2022, I walked along the leafy shoreline of Kona's Ali'i Drive as waves crashed against the guardrail. I noticed a pair of Union Products plastic "Noel" candles standing alongside lighted versions of the Holy Family on the lawn of the small Keala O' Ka Malamalama Church. These stood incongruously next to the dramatic, sword-plunging statue of the Archangel Michael guarding the Catholic church next door, but the candles also reminded me of my New England childhood some forty years and 5,000 miles away. I had forgotten those holiday decorations for years and, when I returned home, I quickly searched online for the value of those vintage candlesticks. A set had recently auctioned for $75—shipping not included—while they never retailed new for more than $10.

The candlesticks and Holy Family sparked my interest in Christmas Americana and eBay drew me into its own commercial wonderland. I found that these plastic ornaments still fetch amazing prices on eBay. That same Santa face Dad hung now sells anywhere from $76 to $220 online, even more than the four-foot Santa with his list or his companion snowman ($60-$180). A pair of gingerbread men listed for $130, but the plastic Jesus, Mary, and Joseph seem in less demand in the secular world, priced under $100 for the set.

In contrast, the first pairs of pink flamingos sold for less than $3 in 1957. In 2020, I paid twelve times that amount for a vintage box set of flamingos in Palm Springs. I laugh to think of attaching Christmas wholesomeness to plastic yard ephemera, but for my family, these treasures from my grandfather remain a part of our tradition. The tradition, however, lasts only from Thanksgiving to January 1–after that, we all agree, lawn decor morphs from "classy to tacky."

Santa's Villages

Just six months after Christmas, our family spent a week's vacation on Maine's coast and a week in New Hampshire's White Mountains. In those mountains lay the pentagon of middle-class family leisure, all connected by the Kancamagus Highway: Clark's Trading Post (since 1928 in Lincoln), Story Land (since 1954 in Glen), both the Conway Scenic Railroad and the Mt. Washington Cog Railway (the latter operating since 1868), and Santa's Village, which opened in 1953 in Jefferson, NH as a summertime Christmas park. Then as now, Story Land and Santa's Village often anchored a New England kid's summer.

Nineteenth-century tourists climbed Mt. Washington with the help of its smoke-billowing cog locomotive while Clark's show bears attracted early motorists with their circus-like animal acts, eatery, and frontier-style gift shop. Relying on interest in the White Mountains' natural beauty and the growing benefits of Ike's Interstate Highway System, Bob and Ruth Morrell built their Story Land with imaginative fairy tale characters in the forests near North Conway. Perhaps the Disney park model of city-sized properties efficiently connected by transportation, or all-inclusive cruise and resort experiences, have thrown much of roadside Americana like this in history's dustbin, but these New Hampshire attractions remain popular.

Drive north on New Hampshire's forested Presidential Highway to reach Santa's summertime village, just two hours from the Canada border. Early in the midcentury, Norman and Cecile Dubois imagined their winter wonderland purportedly after watching prancing deer near their north country home. They opened Santa's Village on Father's Day, June 21, 1953, as a family Christmas park around the same time as other midcentury holiday leisure experiments.

Yule-themed parks proliferated across the country. Santa's Workshop at the North Pole (North Pole, New York) started as one of the earliest Christmas parks when it first welcomed guests on July 1, 1947. Glenn Holland opened a similar park in Skyforest, California in 1955 and then franchised his idea with a second park near Santa Rosa, California in 1957 and a third in Dundee, Illinois in 1959. Santa's Land USA of Putney, Vermont opened independently in 1957, and similar attractions existed in Santa Claus, Indiana and Colorado Springs. Eventually, larger, national and regional theme parks like those of the Walt Disney Company, as well as Dolly Parton's Dollywood and the Six Flags parks, also added seasonal holiday celebrations to their year-round attractions, luring Americans and their dollars for Christmas fun after their summer thrills.

In November 2022, I began receiving envelopes in the mail filled with nostalgic family photos that captured long-forgotten Christmas scenes. The postmarks all read Vermont, and I knew my mother worked hard to try to mitigate my holiday homesickness with these old memories. Like a college freshman, I found myself waiting for the mail to arrive each day. The first packet included old Polaroid photos of a tiny me at Santa's Village. My hunky father could not have been 24 and my heartthrob mom just a year younger. Those high school sweethearts now approach fifty years of marriage with three adult children.

I held the Polaroids by their white labels. The first in the pile showed my beaming mom sitting with me in Santa's sleigh, and the wholesome Village surely made her heart sing.

Santa's Village of Jefferson, NH, c. 1982

Another photo showed me seated in the open hand of a giant cement snowman with Dad standing beside me, preventing a short fall to the ground (see back cover). The snowman has a subtle creepiness with his two thick legs and a svelte belly; yet, nothing says "Santa's Village" like that picture. After posing for the iconic snowman photo, Mom always pushed us towards the life-sized Nativity figures.

Visiting the Nativity barn always felt less fun than, say, sliding down the arms of the giant toy soldier, but Mom mandated the manger visit. I found a picture of me standing beside a camel-riding wise man. Little did I know I would ride camels as a Peace Corps Volunteer in Morocco twenty years later.

I recall a pond by the holy stable, with at least seven swans a-swimming and quite possibly six geese a-laying. Nearby dispensers allowed one to crank out a handful of bird seed for a quarter, like an old gumball machine. Years later, with my brother in tow, I remember feeding the fowl.

"Can I please have a quarter, Dad?" I asked.

Dad will always use pocket change over Apple Pay.

"Crank that handle real good," he said as I inserted the coin.

"And give some of that seed to your brother," Mom added.

My toddler brother saw plenty of folks tossing little grains at the patient birds. Rather than wait for some of mine, he looked down and saw the shore lined with pellets of gray, crushed stone. He helped himself to a free handful of pebbles and, with his strong arm, hurled the shrapnel at Santa's fine feathered friends. In turn, Santa's cygnets swam for the other shore and possibly South Carolina. We left the pond quietly, under the gaze of several nonplussed parents.

In addition to snowmen, camel-riding kings, and birds, woodland animals also populate Santa's Village, including deer and reindeer that served as the Dubois family's inspiration for the park. Mom sent another old photo of me lurching back from a curious fawn. I looked uncomfortably innocent; Santa's forest friends were not my friends. My cousin endured a less happy experience with Santa's deer when one bucked him into the mud. The park refitted him in Santa's Village apparel to salvage the rest of the visit, but a California girl had less luck. According to the *San Bernardino Sun*, a once free-roaming reindeer "gored" the daughter of an employee of Santa's Village near Lake Arrowhead. For those reasons, I intuitively preferred the carousel of prancing reindeer.

A walk around New Hampshire's North Pole passed by the old Post Office, the perfect place to send a letter to Santa, and then the village blacksmith who fit each child with a ring made from a horseshoe nail. In addition to the holy hayloft, we always visited St. Nicholas Chapel. On one trip, I recall Pépère Legere removing his hat as we entered the space–still holy to him even in an amusement park.

The chapel has offered a restful space to visitors since the park's early days in 1954. The altar came from St. Joseph's Church–now Cathedral–in Manchester, New Hampshire. In 1884, Denis Bradley of Ireland knelt before the altar as New Hampshire's first bishop. Five years later, he co-founded my *alma mater*, Saint Anselm College, just outside Manchester. Today, Bradley House stands in his honor on campus. As an undergraduate, I spent many afternoons in Bradley House learning from admirable professors, yet I knew none of that history–nor could I anticipate my college years–as a boy visiting Santa in his village.

At long last, after what seemed an eternity of walking, we arrived at Santa's cottage. Even as a kid, visiting Santa in August seemed peculiar, and I have wondered in the years since if the same Santa moonlighted as Heidi's grandfather at Story Land across the Kancamagus. While the idea seems unlikely, swap Santa's red flannel for Swiss lederhosen and he became the same bearded White Mountains man. Whether in New Hampshire or California, a Santa visit looks the same around the world with the requisite interrogation about behavior and discussion of your itemized shopping list. Sometimes there's some banter about your day in the park before picture taking and a swift exit. Although you visited the Village for Kris Kringle, the park kept a finale even bigger than Santa himself.

Santa's yule flume log ride stood just before the exit gift shop and lured you in from the parking lot. Log-shaped canoes floated through the New Hampshire woods only to climb yet another of the "white mountains" before splashing down in the river below. Then as now, the flume remains cascading fun. Among the old photos Mom sent, I found a typically off-center, and out-of-focus, picture taken by Mémère Legere of my grandfather, brother, and me floating in the log. My grandfather waved while my brother and I wore smiles across our faces, marking the perfect ending to a park day.

By Disney standards, it's a sleepy park, but don't write off Santa's Village; in a 2023 *USA Today* list of America's best Christmas theme parks, Santa's Village of New Hampshire ranked ahead of Dolly Parton's Smoky Mountains Dollywood–where it's surely not a "Hard Candy Christmas." Silver Dollar City in Branson, Missouri, claimed the number-one spot for a Christmas theme park that year.

In Leominster, we enjoy our own "Santa's Village" in miniature. For generations, a small man with a big heart, who lived in a small house on Merriam Avenue, decorated his yard with Christmas statuary that he carved from Styrofoam. Until his death at the age of 104, Louis Charpentier practiced masterful carving. His greatest legacy is likely the life-size wooden crucifix he carved from a single tree to hang over the altar of Saint Cecilia's parish church. His Styrofoam Christmas sculptures looked more whimsical than Christ in agony: a snowman and snowlady, Santa genuflecting before the baby Jesus, tireless (non-union) elves at work, and a Jack-in-the-Box that all shared the visual vocabulary of "Christmas."

When visiting my grandparents in Leominster, we always stopped and walked through Mr. Charpentier's yard display. Sometimes he greeted us from the door and other times he sat comfortably inside. I came to appreciate the experience again in my thirties when I hosted a foster child who also enjoyed the curious collection in his pre-teen years. I loved seeing that sense of young wonder on the boy's face. When Mr. Charpentier died in 2015, his family donated the large collection of crafts to the city, which still displays them annually in City Hall. Plenty of news stories describe similar displays across the country.

Writing thirty years and 5,000 miles away, I am brought back to our Santa's Village vacations as well as the Christmas collection in Mr. Charpentier's yard. I suppose those were precisely the memories my parents and grandparents wanted to give us. In 1955, admission to the Village cost a few dollars, with children under ten admitted free. Twenty years later, the cost for people over four years old only climbed to $3. By my mother's recollection, during our visits in the '80s, entrance cost ten times as much. Today, admission to Santa's Village sits at $45 for an adult while a one-day ticket to Dollywood fetches $92. Compare that to a Disneyland outing costing over $200 some days just to pass the turnstile. As much as I love Disneyland, I am not convinced the experience is any better for the young ones than Santa's Village. My sister and I once overheard an exhausted mom in a Disney park silence her toddler with: "Quiet, or I'll feed you to the Yeti we just saw." At Santa's Village, on the other hand, you only hear a saccharine, "Santa knows if you're naughty or nice," to control behavior.

Dreaming of White Christmases

My sister and I once toured Paramount Studios in Los Angeles after dark. We handled treasured costumes and props as well as walked across the sets that made Hollywood. At the end of the tour, we entered an old movie theater with worn chairs and ancient fabrics. "This room," the guide told us, "saw *The Godfather, Forrest Gump*, and *White Christmas* for the first time. Those movies came alive here." We knew we stood on hallowed ground.

While the charismatic *White Christmas* quartet of Bing Crosby, Rosemary Clooney, Danny Kaye, and Vera-Ellen found Vermont warm and dry on their arrival, I've usually known it white for the holiday. I delight in my winter memories of Vermont, especially when writing from a leafy and rainy Hawaii lanai. Just as the movie contrasts the early Florida scenes with the Vermont finale, I appreciate the similar contrast between Hawaii and the Green Mountains at Christmas.

Ben and I watched *White Christmas* while nursing his flu in 2022. It's my one "must-see" film every Christmas, likely because Mémère Aubuchon loved it. The Haynes sisters sing about "Sisters" and it reminds me of Mémère and her sister, Loretta who, at 91, still keeps us in check with her text messages and our bellies full with her holiday *tourtière* pork pie. Watching

White Christmas with Ben, even with a December Kona rain storm pounding our windows, soothed a bit of my pining for New England pines.

I grew up in the woods but we usually decorated an artificial Christmas tree because of Mom's allergies—a decision that seems somewhat sensible in the face of today's climate crisis. The "big box" contractor stores in Hawaii do sell dead and bundled Christmas trees, but that seems irresponsible given the resources used to ship a tree to the island, the associated mess, and the need to dispose of it in a non-native environment. Instead, Ben and I keep a replica "Charlie Brown Christmas Tree" manufactured under a Peanuts® license. The artificial twig looks just like it did in the cartoon, complete with Linus' light-blue blanket as a tree skirt, and it suits us.

When we lived in California, I loved the holiday build-up in swanky Palm Springs with its twinkle and sparkle. At Christmas, however, Ben and I retreated to our Joshua Tree hideaway in the Mojave desert. Twice I experienced the otherworldly sight of snowfall in Joshua Tree, with snow collecting on the spikes of the trees in the silence of the High Desert. On Christmas, we took long hikes in the National Park, warmed ourselves with mulled wine, watched Christmas movies, and shared a festive meal, maybe even ate a Moroccan *tagine*. Despite being in our forties, we exchanged fun Christmas presents like puzzles and games as well as sweets to eat and spirits to drink. I appreciated the simplicity of Joshua Tree's desert landscape against the glitzy excess of Palm Springs.

Ben surprised me on the morning of our first Christmas Eve in Hawaii.

"Do you want to see a white Christmas?" he asked.

"Oh, this should be good," I returned. "Where? White caps on the ocean waves?"

"Hop in the sleigh, Santa," he said.

He drove north to the Saddle Road beneath the Mauna Kea volcano which, at over 14,000 feet elevation, usually has a snow cap in winter. Park rangers inspected cars for snow chains, which we lacked, so we limited our trip to the visitor's center where we saw the snow well enough. We laughed to see small pickup trucks laden with snow descend from the mountaintop, undoubtedly as a snowy surprise for kids on Christmas Eve. The seasonal rains made the undulating lava fields look more like the rolling green hills of Ireland than Pele's playground. The few hours we spent inland felt unexpectedly like home. Mauna Kea is not Joshua Tree, but I appreciate its own unique contribution to the diversity of the American landscape.

In generations past, Hawaiian silverswords (*argyroxiphium sandwicense*) commonly grew on the slopes of Mauna Kea and Maui's Haleakala volcanoes. These fragile spikes are called *'āhinahina* in *'Ōlelo Hawai'i*, which literally means, "very gray." As the name suggests, the small bushes of metallic-looking silver blades grow no bigger than a head of lettuce. Extraordinary conservation efforts remain underway to preserve the spiky shrubs on the volcano's slope. In looking at the little silvery bushes on Christmas Eve, I could only think of Burl Ives singing "Silver and Gold," although I found nothing particularly festive about the spikes sprouting from the hard lava. Spending Christmas Eve on a volcano ranked among my less traditional holidays, but nothing could ever match the great, silvery surprise of Christmas Eve 1996.

Christmas Eve festivities–in many ways the apex of our family Christmas–followed a non-negotiable schedule each year: the

Nativity pageant Mass, the gathering at my grandparents' house, and back home to bed before Santa arrived. We never deviated from this schedule beginning with the 4:00 liturgy. Imagine my surprise when, at 3:00 on December 24, 1996, my parents called my brother (9 years old) and me (turning 16) into the den where Mom and Dad sat with a two-foot cube wrapped as a present. The gathering felt like a trap.

"We want you to open this present first," Mom said. "It's for both of you."

Our suspicion grew; they clearly set a trap. We never opened presents before seeing Mémère and Pépère Aubuchon, and certainly not before church.

"It's a PlayStation," said my brother, hoping for the 1990s Sony video game console.

"Has to be," I said.

Casting our doubts aside with the torn wrapping paper, we failed to notice the expressions on Mom and Dad's faces.

"Definitely a PlayStation," my brother continued as we broke the tape to open the box, our fingers moving deftly with the adrenaline that pumped through children at Christmas. Think of Ralphie and his BB gun in *A Christmas Story*. This gift, we knew, was The Big One. The reused box beneath the candy-cane-striped paper had contained, if I recall correctly, a crock pot, which signaled more perplexion and more warnings of entrapment.

In our frenzied gift opening, we found no PlayStation and, when we could stand the suspense no longer, up floated a silver Mylar balloon that read in pink letters: "IT'S A GIRL!"

"Where's the PlayStation?" we implored.

My mother's heart broke before us. She, and I'm sure Dad, too, wanted to share their special news about our sister for

Christmas. The sentiment proved too obtuse for two young, and understandably excited, boys. My mother collected herself as all moms do and carefully re-wrapped the balloon. She brought it to Mémère Aubuchon that evening, who in turn opened it in front of the family with glad tidings and great joy. My brother and I made sure to look happy about it the second time around.

Mémère Aubuchon died a few years later, and our family Christmases number among my favorite memories of her–when she was most herself, on Christmas, sharing joy with the whole family. When my mother began sending me old Christmas photographs in the mail, I found a snapshot of my sister with Mémère Aubuchon on Christmas Eve 1997, a year after the great gender reveal. Although Jenn was quite young when Mémère Aubuchon died, she and Mémère Legere enjoyed many years of friendship. How thankful I am to remember that silver balloon every Christmas Eve.

God Rest Ye Merry

When my sister graduated high school, I took her to London to celebrate a Merry Christmas in Merry England. We did all the London things: walked along the Thames, saw Peter Pan fly across the great clock, stared at Harrods' window displays, and even watched the Phantom at a matinee (less seasonal). We also escaped London for a day in Canterbury because nothing says Christmas like a slayed archbishop or a poem of *Tales* with 17,000 lines.

We relished a delightful retreat, or at least one better than Becket's, taking in a bit of country and a lot of medieval England. We did all the pilgrim things: lit our cathedral candles, said our holy prayers, and gave a nod to St. Anselm, whose bones the Protestant Reformers scattered but he was not slayed. All that walking and praying made us pilgrims hungry and thirsty.

At "Tiny Tim's Tearoom" on St. Margaret's Street, we ordered a plowman's lunch as perfect as the Last Supper: mulled wine, bits of cheese and fruit, and fresh scones. The mulled wine warmed the heart as well as the cheeks from the nip of the cool Kent air. At rest, we enjoyed a second glass if not a third. We accomplished all that before heading to the train station and back to London. Rest assured, we merrily found our way home and added mulled wine to our annual menu.

The Little Town of Bethlehem

Much like Mary and Joseph crossing Judea to Bethlehem for the supposed Roman census (it seems Luke named the wrong governor), I also once experienced a desert Christmas as a stranger in Morocco. I traveled from my home in the mountains to the Atlantic coast which, by the early 2000s, looked nothing like Bethlehem in Roman Syria. That Moroccan Christmas, spent in the port city of Agadir, represented the kind of meaningful, ex-pat holiday for which I yearned in my first year in Hawaii.

Morocco embraces a long history of religious pluralism dating back to the expulsion of Jews and Muslims from Spain in the fifteenth century. The seaside hamlet of Essaouira has a Jewish *mellah* with a Jewish cemetery not far from a Catholic chapel, similar to the cities of Marrakech and Fez. The French Protectorate of Morocco brought Catholic priests to the country and they mostly minister in tourist areas. The capital, Rabat, has included the Cathedral of St. Peter and its archbishop since 1919. In the far east of the country, near Midelt, sits the small monastery of Our Lady of the Atlas where the friars and sisters lead simple lives of service to the native mountain people. The brothers built the monastery from the rocks and clay earth to meld the eternal with the created, rather than impose the Gothic on the vulgar as done elsewhere.

In Agadir, the small, warehouse-like church honors St. Anne—recognized as the grandmother of Jesus by both Christian and Muslim traditions. The space feels like a decorated shoe box. Rarely, however, have I seen the zeal of such an aged priest as its pastor, who peppered the French liturgy with a good dose of English and German. Just like at my childhood Christmas pageants, in the solitude of the holy evening, we sang "Silent Night." I never experienced that song in languages other than English and my grandparents' French. That night, we raised our hundred-strong voices in Spanish, German, Dutch, and Korean on the coast of Africa and not far from shepherds tending flocks. I experienced peace there, that abiding peace that comes from the heart rather than the ego.

I love Christmas cards. I have hundreds of cards saved from years past and I re-read many of them as a Christmas tradition. I like cards with beachy Christmas flamingos in Santa hats. I like Snoopy cartoon cards. I like cards with funny jokes about Marvin, the fourth wise man from Miami. One commonly-used Christmas image, however, irks me: middle-aged male shepherds keeping warm at night by a fire circle.

During my time as a Peace Corps Volunteer in Morocco, I lived and worked among the shepherds of southern provinces. I cannot remember seeing a male shepherd but I often saw girls of about thirteen protecting their family's flocks. These girls were too young to marry but had finished elementary school and were sent to tend the sheep. "Boys are too valuable to send to the field" a Moroccan school teacher once explained to me. Given the long and wide vistas that surrounded the village, I often saw the girls walking towards the horizon in the morning and returning in the evening having trod many miles to find verdant scrub for the sheep and goats to graze. You can also forget about a campfire as deforestation and desertification continue to consume the edge of the Sahara.

Into the Sahara by camel, Peace Corps Morocco, c. 2008

The Torah recounts the story of Moses' shepherdess wife, Zipporah, as well as the story of the Jewish matriarch Rachel before her, but in the West we usually assume men shepherd their flocks. The irony applies to Catholic priests and bishops, too. Know that pastoral life in the twenty-first century Sahara is far from charming, and I doubt it looked any more glorious two millennia ago. So please, do send Christmas cards*, but not the ones with the male shepherds.

*Buy UNICEF cards and do some good with your purchase.

O Xmas Tree

Much like the scenes of the Bethlehem story, my favorite adult Christmases have often been quiet. Foremost among them, as I described before, rank our Joshua Tree Christmases, but the Christmas of 2012–a whole decade before the move to Hawaii–stands out in my mind. The year 2012 tasted tart like cranberry relish rather than sweet like gingermen while I settled into my new, divorced life. I planned to visit my family on Christmas, but I felt quite alone that December until I received an invitation from a colleague to visit her and her husband at their new home in northern Vermont. In need of cheer, I accepted their invitation and drove towards Canada just before Christmas.

Kayla and Al's camaraderie became a gift as they opened their home to me as a weary traveler. We strolled through the college town of Burlington under its twinkling lights and fluffy blanket of snow with the kiss of seasonal chill in the air. We nibbled flatbread for dinner and found our way into a neighborhood pub for warm libations and live music. We shared a perfect night and, while a Christmas card represents the extent of our correspondence these days, I recall that December 23 in Burlington with such warmth, along with the reminder to open my own doors to strangers.

O XMAS TREE

Ten years after my chilly Vermont Christmas with Kayla and Al, Ben and I prepared for a 2022 sunset stroll toward the beach for Christmas dinner. Before leaving, I looked back over the old photographs Mom had mailed. The heyday hairstyles and film-frozen fashions brought back fond childhood memories. The sense of place struck me particularly hard: my grandparents' living room with its tinseled tree, our old house in the snowy woods, and the knit stockings hung in Mom and Dad's Vermont house. Now, green trees and the blue of the Pacific paint the image outside our condo windows, but not green like New England's tall conifers. In Joshua Tree, I had twice seen a snowy blanket outside my windows, so even when the land looked dry and brown, I could well imagine it white. I struggled to activate that imagination in Hawaii.

"Merry Christmas, boys," our favorite bartender, Gunnar, said as he gave the Hawaiian shaka gesture. He enjoyed an especially good arms day. "Howzit?"

"We came for an *aperitif*," Ben said before explaining further. "A drink before dinner."

"The regular, please," I said, and Gunnar nodded.

We relaxed, Hawaiian style, during that golden happy hour on "a bright, Hawaiian Christmas day…." We shook hands with our friends and, with cheeks as rosy as Santa, we walked next door to *Huggo's*, the sister restaurant of *On The Rocks*, for our indulgent surf and turf dinner. We looked out over the dark Kailua Bay and saw just a few stars over the sea. The ocean breeze cooled our warm cheeks and the gentle surf replaced Dean and Bing as our soundtrack. The scene recalled neither snowy Vermont nor sunny California, but the Christmas evening was ours, as much as I struggled to see it.

Merry Little Christmas

After two millennia, I am not the only one trying to understand the meaning and relevance of Christmas. Leominster's Union Products Co. closed its doors in 2006, ceasing production not only of its lawn flamingos but also its plastic Santas and snowmen. For two generations they successfully produced unique holiday treasures later eclipsed by cheaper and easier-to-ship inflatable decorations. The Cado Company of neighboring Fitchburg bought the old injection molds and still produces some plastic holiday items from time to time. Those artifacts of my youth may be gone, but they are surely not forgotten as an eBay search attests.

New Hampshire's Santa's Village has remained a family-owned and expanding theme park since 1953, two years before California's Disneyland opened. Similar theme parks have not enjoyed equally-steady business. Glenn Holland's Santa's Village near Lake Arrowhead, California survived for more than thirty years before lying dormant between 1998 and 2016 when it reopened as Skypark at Santa's Village. Skypark kept its mix of outdoor adventure attractions as well as Holland's classic kiddie features, representing a good example of adaptation and reinvention, despite the old news of the girl gored by a reindeer.

Holland's other franchised parks did not enjoy the same

longevity. The Scotts Valley location, near San Francisco, barely survived a decade from 1958-1969 and, while the Dundee, Illinois park remained in operation between 1959 and 2006, it eventually relocated and reestablished itself not as the timeless North Pole but as Santa's Azoosment Park with its "Paintball Explosion" and caged exotic pets, which seem incongruous to the Christmas spirit. Perhaps the New Hampshire Village's fidelity to its theme and mission has secured its enduring legacy.

Santa's Land USA still sits in quiet Putney, Vermont, just fifteen miles from my family's home. The small park opened in 1957 and guidebooks of roadside Americana often list it as a by-way place to visit. My father remembers visiting the park from Massachusetts as a boy in the early 1960s.

"I loved the green Vermont license plates in the parking lot," he told me. Massachusetts–the first state to issue automobile license plates—engraved navy blue plates around 1960 while Vermont has consistently issued green-and-white plates. "I always wanted a green license plate," he told me.

"How about Santa Claus?" I asked.

"Loved him less than the green plates," he responded. He now has a green license plate.

Santa's Land USA closed its doors in 2012 before a local woman announced plans to revive the pine-covered wonderland out of a self-labeled "maternal instinct." She argued that she "couldn't see capitalism destroying family tradition and family values" before she faced animal cruelty charges (see *Vermont Country Magazine*, November 2019). Happily, the park reopened in 2017 and Santa continues to welcome lots of tots to his Vermont home, reinforcing the continuity of these American holiday spaces from the midcentury.

Places and presents often shape our holiday memories and, in being so removed from the familiar places I had known, Hawaii with its palm trees and beaches felt especially far away that Christmas. When I look back at that time from a distance, I recognize all the familiar elements: classic lawn decor, a special landscape, enchanting presents, and memories sparked by old photographs lovingly sent by my mother; I just failed to clearly see them. The things we carry with us–"what the Fates allow" in Judy Garland's *Merry Little Christmas*–much more than the things we leave behind, shape our present and future. We delight at Christmas when we recall as much.

II

Not a Silent Night

*"I believe in Santa Claus, and I'll tell you why I do.
'Cause I believe that dreams and plans
and wishes can come true."*
—Dolly Parton

*I appreciated a sonorous Christmas as the waves
crashed upon Hawaiian sands.*

Hark

I saw the illuminated Christmas tree in Rockefeller Square just once, on a freezing-cold night between Christmas and the New Year, with my sister. We visited the city to see the 2017 finale of the *CATS* revival on Broadway, which did not disappoint. In my mind's eye, I connect the flicker of the lights in the jellicle junkyard to the twinkle on the boughs of the giant tree just down the street. Christmas, for me, has a lot to do with performances. I directed plenty of stage productions, studied dramatic arts in graduate school, and can say with certainty that my appreciation of theater started on Christmas Eve 1987, in St. Denis Church, Ashburnham, Massachusetts with Mrs. Joan Webber directing.

Mrs. Webber has all the expertise of a stage mom and teacher combined. For more than seventy-five years since becoming a Brownie Scout in 1946, she has tirelessly given back to her community and church. Much like Maria von Trapp, Mrs. Webber has six children and often taught–whether Girl Scouts or catechism students like me–while strumming her guitar. Her husband, Mr. Bill Webber, taught in the high school math department for many years and, with his white beard, has always volunteered as Santa's helper in our small town. Every year, when tasked by the pastor to assemble the students for the Christmas Eve pageant, Mrs. Webber did so with the enthusiasm of a Girl Scout leader, and she perfected its staging as only a mother could.

To avoid anxiety over forgotten lines, Mrs. Webber limited pageant dialogue to just the Announcing Angel, played by an aged sixth grader. Everyone else comprised a holy (and silent) tableaux. Older students dressed as Mary, Joseph, and the three Magi. All the other boys dressed in terry cloth bathrobes as shepherds while the girls wore white dresses and garland-lined white cardboard angel wings. Keep in mind, this was the 1980s and I do not doubt that if a parent or child had a problem playing a gendered shepherd or angel, kindly Mrs. Webber had a solution ready. I dare say she's more pragmatic than any pope.

Mrs. Webber told the boys to bring a nice broomstick or straight branch to use as a shepherd's staff. To my surprise, just before we headed to church on that Christmas Eve, Pépère Aubuchon, the woodworking St. Joseph of our family, arrived at our house with a shepherd's crook for me. The rustic and hand-carved crosier would have won the envy of JP2 as it pulled strays back into the fold. I quickly showed Mrs. Webber when I arrived with it in hand.

"My Pépère carved this so I'd look like a real shepherd," seven-year-old me beamed.

"And don't you look the part?" she replied before herding us into our positions. She looked like the woman who lived in a shoe, who had so many children she didn't know what to do … except Mrs. Webber knew what to do.

That evening, the adult lector read the Christmas story as Mary and Joseph walked down the aisle of the packed country church. In its simplicity, St. Denis exists at a distance from the world's great cathedrals with their stained glass and gilded ornaments. Yet, that simplicity placed the spiritual focus of the evening on the children performers. The Announcing Angel appeared at the lectern to bring "good news of great joy." The giggling girls processed into the sanctuary (stage left) while the boys–either serious or bored–did the same thing on the other side. We all sang "Silent Night" and before you could hum alleluia, we changed from our costume and headed home to await Santa. The magic of the St. Denis Christmas pageant, without question, stemmed from Mrs. Webber's expert ability to stage a fabulous and faithful fifteen-minute show.

My years on the stage passed and I rose through the theatrical ranks from "Shepherd 17" to "Shepherd 6" to "King 3" to "Joseph" and that crowning achievement, the "Announcing Angel." I still remember my line from St. Luke (talk about a playwright!): *"Do not be afraid; for behold, I proclaim to you good news of great joy that will be for all the people. For today in the city of David a savior has been born for you who is Lord. And this will be a sign for you: you will find an infant wrapped in swaddling clothes and lying in a manger."* I must confess, Linus from the Peanuts® gang recited it better on TV than I did.

I had little dramatic interest in high school or college, and only stepped back on stage as a young teacher. Years later, after returning to teach at my high school *alma mater*, I took up the director's stage chair and produced the most loved musical of all time–*The Sound of Music*–which reminded me, of course, of Mrs. Webber. Imagine my astonishment when, after the curtain closed on the last night of that production, I greeted Mr. and Mrs. Webber, sitting in the front row.

"We haven't missed an Oakmont show since 1960," she said.

"You gave me my start," I reminded her. "As a tiny shepherd with a crook. Thank you for that," I said as we hugged.

It's Christmastime in ... Disney

I have not visited Santa's Village in decades, but as an adult, my Christmases have become tied to that stronghold of Americana–Florida's Walt Disney World Resort. Twice as a kid–in December of 1992 and 1996—I traveled with the Oakmont marching band to the Magic Kingdom to parade through the park. I have fond memories of the park decorated for Christmas in its exaggerated style while our Marching Spartans passed Cinderella's castle and marched down Main Street, USA.

Twenty years later, I found myself back at Oakmont as a teacher and a close friend of the school's new band leader, Kris DeMoura. In 2012, 2015, and 2018–I made weekend trips to cheer on Kris and the band from the Magic Kingdom's sidewalk. Although by 2021 I had moved from Massachusetts to California, I still planned to visit both with Kris and the band as well as my good friends Danielle and Rob (and their son Parker) who had relocated to the Orlando area. When another COVID variant surged in 2021, Kris postponed that trip a whole year to 2022, after I moved to Hawaii. The expense of that trip–no longer a quick east coast weekend break–coupled with the expenses of moving to Hawaii, made the 2022 trip seemingly impossible.

Kris and I taught together for nearly ten years; he was the Rodgers to my Hammerstein. In many ways, moving away from him was harder than moving away from my work at Oakmont. I confessed to him that I had no reasonable way to travel to Orlando for a short weekend as I did before. Kris assured me he understood completely, but my melancholy metastasized as I wouldn't see my friends, Danielle and Rob, either. This would hardly read like a Christmas story with that sad ending.

I soon cracked; I could not disappoint my friends. Exactly one week before the Florida parade, I paid for my airfare, rental car, and park tickets. Then I texted Kris:

Jeff: *"No joke, but I just booked my flight for Disney. I just didn't feel right not going. A day will come when I can't, but not yet."*

Kris: *"I'm speechless. Really. I really appreciate it, but you didn't have to. And happy that you'll get to see the band. And us."*

I expected both physical and financial exhaustion from my travel, but I remained undaunted. The emotional boost of seeing my friends would offset the fatigue, I reckoned. Although I struggled to find Christmas in Hawaii, if anyone can make you believe anything, even that you can fly like Peter Pan, it's the folks at Walt Disney World. Ben could not leave work with such short notice, but he encouraged me to go and reconnect with my friends in an attempt to nurse away my sadness. The plan included flying all night to meet my friends at the park by 8 am, staying for the day, crashing at Danielle's house, and flying out the next morning for the twenty-two-hour journey back to Kona. If Santa could fly around the world in twenty-four hours, surely I could make it to Florida and back in forty-eight.

Imagine both my surprise and satisfaction when I arrived at the park before the band! I felt like the boy Pinocchio without strings. I could walk where I pleased and see what I wanted. I got myself a much-needed coffee from Starbucks on Main Street, USA and walked under the fruit-laden garlands and holiday wreaths that adorned the street lamps. *Disney World looks more festive than the North Pole,* I thought. I strolled past the statue of Walt and Mickey and onward through Cinderella's castle–straight on to Neverland!

Well, straight on to the ride Peter Pan's Flight. The line looked short so I entered but, unlike the attraction's California version, where the winding line bends in front of the attraction, the Florida version winds its way through the hidden halls of the Darling family home and into the children's nursery before climbing aboard the flying dream ships on the way to Neverland. The delightful nursery diorama helps pass the waiting time but also hides the length of the queue. A family of four walked in front of me, mesmerized by Tinkerbell's appearance in the nursery, and then by the sight of the flying ships. *Holidays and dreams come from children like them*, I mused. Once aboard, we soared over London and onto Neverland, above the Jolly Roger and the mermaid lagoon not unlike Santa in his sleigh. Of all of Disney's magical inventions, none ever pleased me like Peter Pan's Flight.

When I returned to *terra firma* I met Danielle and Parker who led me on a grand tour of the park–from the Seven Dwarves' mine to Space Mountain to the Caribbean pirates and Wonderland's tea cups. We laughed and we lost ourselves in the youthfulness that Walt Disney envisioned for his playground. I can think of few Christmas gifts sweeter than that.

Just as we walked through Fantasyland we spotted none other than Peter Pan himself!

"I need to borrow Parker," I said to Danielle.

"Okay, okay," the boy said obligingly as we waited not to see jolly old Saint Nick but a much younger elf.

I pushed Parker ahead of me to watch Peter Pan enthrall the twelve-year-old. The sprite never broke character and he talked in Peter's quick, rough manner. Peter took his time with each guest and had something unique to say to everyone who waited to see him. I found a lesson in our experience: no matter how boring, or how tiring, being jolly means making the visitor feel special with unbroken eye contact, right at the kid's height. *Santa*, I told myself, *does the same.* Danielle took our photo (I looked twice his age) and I sent it to Ben with a note: *now there's a cheerful elf to put on the shelf.*

Our park festivities paused for the Marching Spartans' parade. Danielle, Parker, and I joined with parents, former students I missed greatly, and colleagues from the school at which Danielle and I had taught. The stretched smiles were genuine, the hugs and hellos meaningful, and, while not specific to Christmas, the feeling of reconnecting, gathering, and celebrating with joy encircled us like a balsam wreath in our shared mission to encourage these students and their teachers.

We heard the drums' cadence and the resounding blast of the tubas long before we saw the flag twirlers. I remembered the spectators lining the park avenues when performing in the same parade as a kid. Our assembled family cheered, whistled, hooted, and hollered—almost overpowering the band—in a moment of surprising joy I find hard to describe, like waking to an unexpected snow day, or scoring the game-winning point, or passing the test that once seemed impossible. Kris naturally exudes optimism, yet, in the four times I saw him and his students parade down Main Street with Cinderella's castle as a backdrop, he radiates happiness and joy that only Santa matches.

That moment included all of those feelings and more.

Faster than the fall of a shooting star, the world's serious problems seemed to pause and our little fellowship shared joy before the parade passed us by. The day-long travel and the $1400 I spent for that instant were wholly and unquestionably worth every penny. Besides, what's more in the spirit of a capitalist Christmas than canoodling your card's credit limit?

"Fantastic stuff, my friend!" I exclaimed, embracing Kris afterward. "Now, you can enjoy that well-earned feeling of relief."

"Yes," he said before moving on to the next task. "How 'bout a Dole Whip?"

"Absolutely," I replied as we walked towards the Enchanted Tiki Room.

We savored ice cream with pineapple juice *sans rhum* and Kris shared some of the details of the band's time backstage. This tour–already postponed a year by COVID–presented more challenges for him and the kids than previous trips. Even with such an outstanding performance, the road to Main Street, USA proved more difficult to walk than before. Kris and I knew the coronavirus world continued evolving, and we probably both wondered about the challenges of the experience three years in the future, but I chose not to dwell on such serious thoughts during our remaining time at Disney World.

We embarked on the Jingle (not Jungle) Cruise, paid our spectral respects at the Haunted Mansion, and sailed through a tired-looking Small World. I write "tired-looking" because some of the animatronic child dolls were not fully operational.

"That hula dancer has a bad hip," Kris laughingly pointed out as we floated through the Pacific.

"Thank God for Obamacare," I said, making us both laugh.

When we stepped from the small world into the world of fantasy, Cinderella's clock struck the fateful hour that signaled my departure. Kris, his family, and the band planned to return to the Magic Kingdom the next day while I flew 5,000 miles west back home to my life with Ben.

I am used to Kris' hugs, although I am not quite a hugger myself, but he surprised me when he said, "I love you, my friend," without jest.

"I love you, too," I said and turned to leave as teardrops

clouded my eyes.

Saying goodbye to Danielle and her family proved no easier in the morning.

"We're going to Disneyland Paris this summer, if you want to join us," she said.

The offer lifted my heavy heart and I knew we would enjoy ourselves. I visited Paris several times before but never to Disneyland Paris as I had thought of it as a bit of a blight on the City of Lights.

"Thanks," I said. "I doubt I can budget for Disneyland Paris this year, but I'll see."

"You always find a way," she said.

"Maybe Peter Pan will sprinkle a little pixie dust on me so I can fly, eh Parker?"

He smiled, perhaps a bit bashfully as a middle schooler, as we bumped fists and I started my long flight to Hawaii, fortified by the holiday embraces of familiar friends.

Christmas Vacation

Profitable Christmas movies have become a genre all their own. I took twenty-five popular holiday movies and categorized them in a librarian-like way to see where my story of Big Island Santa fits. As these movies only tell a handful of stories over and over again, I wonder if my contribution of yet another story to the Christmas canon has any merit? Please note, I am only working with major motion pictures, not the dime-a-dozen Christmas flicks from the Hallmark Channel as they offer special joy to the world.

At its heart, the Christmas story tells a ghost tale far more spooky than yule. Dickens' *A Christmas Carol*, best adapted to the screen with *Mickey's Christmas Carol* (1983) and *The Muppets Christmas Carol* (1992), remains the benchmark for all Christmas stories. Add to this list another Disney ghost story: Tim Burton's *The Nightmare Before Christmas* (1993), which exists at the curious confluence of claymation, Christmas, and Halloween. Include the many filmed versions of Tchaikovsky's *The Nutcracker* for their sweet sugar plum dreams, nut-cracking hero, and a Rat King who reigned long before the American mouse. If you want to talk about the supernatural myths surrounding the Nativity story, then consider *The Greatest Story Ever Told* (1965) or, equally compelling, *Monty Python's Life of Brian* (1979). All of these Christmas stories deal with the great beyond as much as poor babies in mangers or Victorian poorhouses.

As early as nineteenth-century London, stories of "diversity and inclusion" have stood adjacent to Christmas ghost stories. Poor Bob Cratchit and his lame son tried to fit in with his industrial neighbors as much as George Bailey tried to fit in with prosperous post-war America. *The Grinch Who Stole Christmas* (1967), *Rudolph the Red-Nosed Reindeer* (1969), *Edward Scissorhands* (1990), and, of course, the misfit *Elf* (2003) all recount stories of outcasts. Christmas, it seems, points out who's different and how to bring them in for a slice of fruitcake.

For all their spectral storytelling, Christmas movies also wrestle with the grim, capitalist realities of personal finance, estate planning, and even environmental policy. Notice some of the oldest and most famous films: *Christmas in Connecticut* (1945), *It's a Wonderful Life* (1946), *Miracle on 34th Street* (1947), and my favorite, *White Christmas* (1954) provide a primer on real estate, life insurance, the judicial system, and show business like a Suze Orman financial seminar. Add to that *Merry Christmas Charlie Brown* (1965), *Mame* (1974), and *Scrooged* (1988) for an indictment of capitalism so fierce it stirs Jacob Marley, Karl Marx, and the gift-giving Magi from their graves. While the world today easily turns a blind eye toward the increasing wealth gap in our neighborhoods and schools, at least some realize our situation in the industry-fueled climate crisis. Don't believe me? Watch *White Christmas* and *Frosty the Snowman* (1969) and tell me I'm wrong about snowfall. Bing Crosby and Jimmy Durante sensed a warming world long before the polar bears told us.

Hollywood blockbusters also rank among favorite festive

films. *Die Hard* (1988) as well as Bruce Willis' other holiday spectacle *RED* (2010) and *Home Alone* (1990) certainly make the "big budget/small substance" list. The Harry Potter movies usually include a charming Christmas scene at the midpoint. *Love Actually* (2003) is an important UK holi-rom-com representing the epitome of the hetero Christmas love story. It's also the epitome of the gay Christmas love story, which affords a convenient congruence. Lastly, no Hollywood Xmas Flicks list is complete without Tom Hanks (*Polar Express*, 2004) and the Academy's favorite Jew, Stephen Spielberg (*Gremlins*, 1984). Mel Brooks (who, surprisingly, never besmirched the holiday genre) closely follows Spielberg as Hollywood's second-favorite Jew. Much like Hanks and Spielberg need inclusion on this list, so, too, does that great American heroine, Dolly Parton, and her *Best Little Whorehouse in Texas* (1982). If you doubt *Whorehouse* is a Christmas movie, watch it and hear Dolly's song *Hard Candy Christmas*, which went gold that year. You will also see dozens of yummy sweet buns perfect for Christmas morning.

While you could file *Big Island Santa* on the capitalism-gone-wild shelf, I propose one final category: Historical Documentary. A collection of Christmas movies exists that illuminates American middle-class family life (include *Gremlins* and *Home Alone* here, too). *A Christmas Story* (1983) along with *National Lampoon's Christmas Vacation* (Chevy Chase, 1989) open the frost-covered windows of our neighbors' parlors and kitchens to show the holiday festivities next door. To the librarians reading: let's keep *Big Island Santa* among these thinly-veiled fictions of American life.

Palm Springs' style centers around the sleek architecture of Midcentury Modernism. I never tired of ambling through the stylish neighborhoods, especially at Christmastime, to see the lavish lighting displays, like a flamboyance of illuminated flamingos on a manicured green lawn. In a city known for its gay culture, these design divas don't disappoint their neighbors. Neither do they next door in Cathedral City where you can stroll down the stellar "Candy Cane Lane." When we last visited in 2021, we found just one resident on the street who kept his house dark—imagine what the neighbors call him.

Listening to Palm Springs' 107.3 Mod FM enhances the search for Christmas lights. Mod FM returns classic midcentury songs to the airwaves in the town made famous by Sinatra's Rat Pack. Indeed, Irving Berlin wrote "White Christmas" against the snow-capped Mount San Jacinto and Bing Crosby's "Blue Skies" Village mobile home park sits on Highway 111. A major thoroughfare bears the name of Gene Autry, without whom we would miss "Rudolph the Red-Nosed Reindeer," along with "Here Comes Santa Claus," and "Up on the Rooftop"–can you imagine such a Christmas? Plenty of bungalows in town still hang sapphire lights for Elvis' "Blue Christmas" too.

Even though I think of Sinatra, Martin, and Davis taking on the Las Vegas New Year's Eve celebrations in the original *Ocean's 11* (1960), their legacy remains entrenched in Palm Springs, especially at the old Beachcomber's (now Bootlegger) tiki club. I cannot imagine Christmas radio without Sinatra's "Have Yourself a Merry Little Christmas," Dean Martin's "Marshmallow World," or Sammy Davis Jr's "Sweet Gingerbread Man." These guys are the soundtrack to Palm Springs living, especially during the holidays. With its lights, snow-capped backdrop, and relaxing radio, I effortlessly embraced the holiday spirit in Palm Springs. Whenever and wherever the radio plays "My Favorite Things" from *The Sound of Music*, I think back to the Webbers and their Christmas lessons. In Hawaii, however, we hear one song more than any other.

Exotica master Art Lyman wasn't the only musician to wish American listeners *Mele Kalikimaka*; in fact, we probably better remember that Irishman Bing Crosby with his 1949 version of the song written by his golf buddy R. Alex Anderson, or when the song plays through Chevy Chase's mind as he looks out his snowy Chicago window and dreams of a new summer pool. Whereas Bing's other hit, "White Christmas," longs for a snowy day, it's the reverse in "Mele Kalikimaka,"

> "Here we know that Christmas
>   Will be green and bright
>   The sun to shine by day
>   And all the stars at night."

Bing's "Mele Kalikimaka" remains the gold standard for the song, but I prefer Bette Midler's cover. As she's Hawaiian-born herself, Midler knows a thing or two about tropical Christmases, even if her Jewish parents lived in Honolulu's predominantly-Asian Aiea neighborhood. Midler graduated from Radford High School where classmates voted her both "most talkative" and "most dramatic" before attending the University of Hawaii at Manoa for three semesters. She made her cinematic debut as an extra in the 1966 film based on Michener's *Hawaii* before heading to New York to embrace fame. Her rendition of "Mele Kalikimaka" hits a bit more on the mark than Bing's. Yet, even with her admonition that Christmas in Hawaii "will be green and bright," I had spent plenty of Christmases in non-snowy climates and wished for something different from my Hawaiian holiday.

At Christmas 2023, Cher released her first rockin' holiday album: *Christmas*. Like most things Cher, the album sounded pretty perfect and *Billboard* named *Christmas* the top-selling seasonal collection of 2023. While my mind perhaps thinks of SoCal more than the Big Island when I listen to her tracks, it's still an up-beat, feel-good, warm-weather kind of album that made my second Christmas in Hawaii a little more spirited.

During the Christmas before shipping out for my Peace Corps service in Morocco, I assured myself that I understood and appreciated the burden placed on the developing world at that time of year. Convinced of my understanding, I routinely played Bob Geldof's 1984 celebrity collaboration for charity: "Do They Know It's Christmas?" The song raised some $10 million for famine relief in Ethiopia.

On my arrival in Morocco (which, I know is not Ethiopia), I fully expected to find, as the song claimed, "a world of dread and fear / Where the only water flowing / Is the bitter sting of tears." Even if you give credit for artistic license, the West's picture of the developing world remains woefully inadequate, especially at Christmas. Yet, forty years later, Geldof's song still plays at Christmas, with a re-release in 2014 to raise awareness for West Africa's Ebola crisis. The song has merit, but unfortunately the West continues harnessing pastoral images of the developing world in an attempt to–perhaps–feel a kinship with the "other" at the holidays.

For me, Christmas is incomplete without reading Dylan Thomas' midcentury recollection of *A Child's Christmas in Wales*. "All the Christmases roll down towards the two-tongued sea like a cold and headlong moon bundling down the sky that was our street," Thomas wrote. In Hawaii, I do look down the hill toward the wide-mouthed sea and Thomas' snow-dusted childhood memories of Wales have become as ubiquitous for my Christmas as much as Dickens' London.

In 2022, when I unpacked some Christmas things and opened the well-worn paper cover of *A Child's Christmas in Wales*, out slid an embroidered white and pink bookmark I gave my grandmother as a Christmas gift. I bought it for her at a Moroccan school for disabled students that taught handicraft skills like embroidery as workplace training; the school was a truly hope-filled place. Mémère Legere read voraciously and, after she died, the bookmark came back to me. I count it among my favorite things to find again every Christmas, and it reminds me there's more hope in the developing world than many know at Christmas.

Books, songs, cards of poor shepherds, and even photographs from tourists and well-meaning Peace Corps Volunteers alike still smack of "poverty porn" to make donors feel good about their year-end tax-deductible "gifts." Charity for a tax deduction, although probably not made with the greatest intention, still tries to alleviate the plight of the poor. Systemic realignment of the global economic order would be a better fix, but opening our door to a neighbor in need—the principal act of charity in the Nativity story—persists as a precious gift, whether in Bethlehem or Beverly Hills.

Joy to the World

Early in December 2022, the Kona Choral Society gave us our first taste of Christmas in Hawaii with their "Joy to the World" concert at St. Michael's Church. We expected an older assortment of well-meaning community members and ex-nuns singing some Christmas classics. We were wrong, and I knew something special would happen when the choir entered singing a traditional Zambian song, "Bonse Aba." With more than 100 singers of diverse ages and with a repertoire just as varied, they sang old favorites with sing-along numbers, as well as songs from Africa and Latin America as part of their joyful anticipation of Christmas. When the choir sang "Silent Night" in five languages: German, Japanese, Spanish, Hawaiian, and English, the music brought me back to that seaside Christmas in Morocco. The evening left such an impression that I marked my calendar for the choir's just-before-Christmas presentation of Vivaldi's *Gloria* and selections from Handel's *Messiah*.

Our family lacks a musical ensemble and mine was among the few male voices in our high school chorus. Still, I can read music and can match my voice to pitches. My years of band practice resulted in a basic, yet solid, understanding of tempo, rhythm, harmony, and a reasonable vocabulary of Italian musical terms like *giocoso* and *sospirando*. In 1995, our chorus teacher, Mr. Blackwell, pushed us to sing a notable portion of Handel's *Messiah,* which my family lovingly remembers as "the high school concert that lasted forever. And ever. And ever." My musical knowledge and appreciation expanded, quite substantially, during my four years at Saint Anselm College in New Hampshire.

Saint Anselm is a traditional liberal arts college run by Benedictine monks. The cylindrical Abbey Church stands at the center of campus both physically and metaphysically, and the College Choir played a significant role in the liturgical life of the school. Father Bede Camera, OSB, the choirmaster in my day, embraced eccentricity. For many years he taught a college course on the scholarship of creativity and always challenged students to see the world uniquely while through a decidedly-Christian lens. As choirmaster, Father Bede knew his notes; he trained at Princeton's Westminster Choir College and collaborated with the estimable American hymnist Alice Parker on the composition of the College Anthem (with words by my friend Fr. Augustine Kelly, OSB). Bede is a good teacher and a good monk, and he imparted three beliefs about singing that I carry whether as a congregant or chorister.

1. Music is born from silence and returns to silence; we *make* music when we separate from the noise of our world.
2. Singing–as prayer–is the only known activity of Heaven (says the Bible). As such, it's a holy endeavor.
3. Only angels "wing" a performance; we must practice like athletes. God is listening.

Fr. Bede taught us to sing master works like Vivaldi and parts of

Messiah as well as a contemporary repertoire that we performed at the weekly student mass and for special occasions like the graduation Baccalaureate Mass. Saint Anselm lacks a robust music program, but when I attended (and probably today), the choir offered students a sense of belonging and a shared mission. In hearing the Kona Choral Society that December, I longed for that sense of belonging and shared endeavor I knew so well in the college choir.

Classical music, such as that of the Kona Choral Society, or what we sang at Saint Anselm, does not please all ears. Once, as we watched a televised performance of *Messiah*, Mémère Legere said to me: "It's nice but how about a jingle bell or a 'ho, ho, ho' every once in a while?" Still, I have spent a fair amount of yuletide with Handel, from high school to college and also enjoyed Handel and Haydn Society concerts at Boston's Symphony Hall and the Master Chorale's *Messiah* at Walt Disney Concert Hall in Los Angeles. The Kona Choral Society performance at Grace Community Church rivaled any of these, with an orchestra of thirty-six instruments.

I knew from their "Joy to the World" concert that the Kona Choral Society represented an admirable amateur venture. Artistic Director Susan Duprey McCreally, who also studied at Westminster Choir College like Fr. Bede, along with the members of the orchestra certainly brought polish and refinement to the community project but, from the first note of Vivaldi to the applause that followed the "Hallelujah Chorus," I knew that the ensemble *makes* music in the way Fr. Bede described. The experience felt like a homecoming.

Similar to other island houses of worship, the walls of Kona's Community Church stand open, making the *al fresco* structure more like a *plein-air* pavilion than a traditional walled sanctuary.

This construction not only circulates air but also invites the sounds and sights of Creation into the worship space. The western side of Grace Church overlooks the Pacific while on the eastern side stands a wall of green mountain foliage that shelters its resident coqui frogs. The constructed formality of Symphony Hall or Walt Disney Hall was kept intentionally away from this space, and yet, the music there still sung right to the soul.

The incongruous surroundings–the views, sounds, and space we collectively filled–stood in even sharper contrast when rain began to fall. This rain would frighten Noah himself. As if cued from heaven, the largest drops fell in abundance when the choir sang "And He shall reign for ever and ever…." That day, even Ben found it hard to dispute that the divine both reigned and rained. Neither Susan nor the chorus nor orchestra seemed to miss a note in the storm–a feat more impressive than the repertoire itself. *I want to be a part of that,* I thought as the chorus intoned the final "Hallelujah."

Before I Melt Away

My Vermont mother sounded concerned when I mentioned our Thanksgiving dinner.

"We're going to a traditional luau," I said. "A big spread of food and then dancing."

"Turkey?"

"No, pork."

"Pork for Thanksgiving, eh? With pineapple, I bet," she added. "And cherries on top."

I think she mentioned cherries as a bit of a dig, but we shared a good laugh. While a luau is not her traditional turkey meal, she appreciated that I live in a new place with new customs. These customs were not wholly new to Mom and Dad who visited Oahu in the 1990s after winning a radio sweepstakes. If only we could find an old photo of Dad hula dancing on Waikiki Beach.

The few people we knew on the island seemed to mark the holiday differently with unique understandings of family, called *'ohana* in *'Ōlelo Hawai'i* (the Hawaiian language). A Japanese-born colleague made traditional Asian foods while a doctor friend delighted in sharing a bucket of the Colonel's fried chicken with her own *'ohana*. Another couple, new to the island like us, roasted a turkey for the first time and feasted for days.

Insofar as the island Thanksgiving looked and tasted different, the experience felt much the same as I knew in New England with food, friends, family, and fellowship at the core. Much to the delight of my mother, the hotel added mashed potatoes and turkey to their traditional luau offerings that night.

Along with a turkey Thanksgiving, I remember hefty piles of snow as a New England boy in the 1980s. When the deck light hit the falling flakes outside just the right way, I could expect a snow day in the morning. As a grown-up teacher, precision forecasting enabled superintendents to call off classes the night before, robbing children (and teachers) of the last-minute bliss of school cancellation. In Hawaii, weather forecasters also called for snow in the mountain elevations just after Thanksgiving 2022 when the Big Island's Mauna Loa erupted for the first time in forty years and dusted parts of the island with white volcanic ash. I laughed hearing a radio broadcaster remind listeners that 'all schools remain open and all pupils are expected to attend,' despite the lightly-falling dust. So much for a Hawaiian snow day.

In New England, snow days meant shoveling, and even now, in my forties, my parents remind me how unenthusiastically I dug out. While not a skier, my friends and I built forts, tunnels, and bobsled channels in the woods around our houses. Climate change robs kids of that fun, and I suspect video games and the Internet are also notable thieves, but living in the tropics presents a wholly-different attitude towards a white Christmas.

Like the balloon that heralded the birth of my sister, few memories of Christmas gifts stick with me some thirty-five years later and, interestingly, I remember the earlier Christmas mornings more than the later ones. The Christmas gift-giving tradition stems from the story of three "wise men" or Magi traveling to Bethlehem to honor the Christ child. One legend holds, and I saw the iconography in the city of Axum illustrating, that all three Magi traveled from Ethiopia. Another legend argues the three Ethiopian Magi were among the first coffee drinkers, as they needed the East African brew to stay awake on their road trip to Bethlehem—giving rise to the customary gift of Starbucks or Dunkin's holiday cards. Tradition also holds that the son of Ethiopia's Queen, known as the Queen of Sheba, smuggled the Ark of the Covenant out of Israel and it remains concealed in Axum to this day. But who really wants an ark for Christmas besides Indiana Jones?

When I was in the first grade, Santa left a tiny, 50 cc, four-wheeler (all terrain vehicle, ATV) by the tree. My stupefaction persists as to how he got the little machine down the chimney. Over the years, that ATV put on more miles than most cars. In second grade, Santa brought me—and many other boys in 1987—a slot car race track. I lacked the subtle dexterity to control the car's speed with the handheld device and my racer derailed at every turn; Dad and I laughed trying to work it, though. Third grade, however, was THE year, like the year when Ralphie got his BB gun in *A Christmas Story*.

For Christmas 1988, Santa delivered a coveted HO model train set. My carpenter dad set two sawhorses in my bedroom with a sheet of plywood covered in green faux-grass paper. At age 8, I could link the 16.5-millimeter rails together as well as the train cars, but I needed help building the model houses for the town. I wanted to build a neighborhood like Mr. Rogers' with his red trolley making its way to the Land of Make-Believe. The train brought me back to our family summer vacations in New Hampshire's White Mountains when, in addition to visiting Santa in his Village, we boarded the historic Conway Scenic Railroad or the Mt. Washington Cog. I wore a striped conductor's cap and overalls for the trip. Years later, when driving across the country to California, I passed long lines of train cars marked Union Pacific and BNSF (Burlington Northern and Santa Fe), representing the adult-size versions of the train cars from my childhood memories.

After the model train and aside from the balloon, I have no memories of receiving particular gifts on the particular holidays that followed. A fancy sled arrived one year and a spyglass another. I never asked Santa for a car as a teenager and, apart from the slot cars mentioned above, the only cars I received at Christmas came as a wood block. Santa (we all knew the Cubmaster played the part) visited our Cub Scout Pack meeting every December and gave each of us scouts a wrapped box with a kit including a block of wood to carve a race car for the annual Pinewood Derby. As trite as it sounds, the event must have been rather special because I can remember those moments so clearly all these years later.* Perhaps the specific details of gifts were lost when the stories I knew of Santa Claus, like those from Ethiopia, passed from history to legend to myth.

---

*We took the Pinewood race seriously in my family as my dad and both grandfathers were carpenters. Perhaps I remember the stress of the race rather than the joy.

If the Fates Allow

Santa's visit to my grandparents' living room marked the summit of the Aubuchon Christmas Eve festivities. The back cover of this book has a photo of me with Santa at that moment. Only later I learned that Santa skipped the other kids' holiday parties, thereby making ours extra special. My search for Christmas on the Big Island grew from this exceptionalism fostered by my grandparents, ma Tante (my aunt) Loretta, and her husband Andy who waxed his mustache *exactly* like Saint Nick.

My grandparents welcomed everyone to their home on Christmas Eve–extended family, boyfriends, girlfriends, and even friends or distant acquaintances with nowhere else to go. My cousins and I were of a similar age, and there's no shortage of old photographs showing us laughing from our bellies (see page 4). Sure, I remember the decorations, food, and gifts, but I never forgot the act of inclusion during the holidays, and I suppose it ranks among my family's most important lessons.

True to her Acadian roots, Mémère Aubuchon and her sister, Loretta, made sure we had plenty of old-country food, too: *tourtière* (pork pie), *râpée*, and *poutines*. Our Acadian poutines consisted of softball-sized meat-filled boiled potato dumplings. These are in contrast to the french fries with cheese curds that some call *poutine* elsewhere in Canada. Pépère Aubuchon called ours "dirty snowballs." My grandmother died more than twenty years ago but my aunts, cousins, and even ma Tante Loretta still prepare those traditional dishes for us. For all the kalua pork in Hawaii, nothing beats ma Tante Loretta's pork pie; I hope similar family dishes laden your table, too.

Ma Tante Loretta, la chef de tourtière et de râpée, c. 1980

Despite all these happy memories I recalled during that first Big Island Christmas, I received some somber news from the mainland. That December, the family veterinarian in Vermont reduced Mom's long-suffering Yorkshire Terrier, Molly, to a diet of just plain rice. Her tiny organs struggled to process rich food. Meanwhile, Ma Tante Loretta sent my father home with a few slices of her coveted, holiday pork pie. When he arrived home, Dad set the pie down to unlace his boots and forgot about the heavenly dish. Later, Mom found Molly asleep next to pie crumbs "as dreams of sugar plums danced in her head." Molly slept for a few days until she embarked on that "long winter's nap" that eventually comes for us all. Mom nursed a broken heart that season but kept a good perspective about Molly's many jolly Christmases. The Fates had cut Molly's string, as the myth says.

Rich Kona coffee, chocolate, macadamia nuts, and vanilla flowers all adore the Big Island's climate and make a Hawaiian Christmas indulgent. A close read of the package of coffee beans in our cupboard shows that less than a quarter of the beans come from Kona. A pound of pure Kona peaberry coffee beans retails for $70, so we buy blended coffee. Instead of coffee, I ship boxes of chocolate-covered Mauna Loa macadamia nuts to New England as seasonal gifts. The market for quality, handmade, small-batch, and locally-sourced chocolates continues to grow on the island with some bars reaching ninety percent of locally-grown bitter cacao. Like island chocolatiers, the Hawaiian Vanilla Company has moved to a more intimate retail experience for confectioners having previously only wholesaled their product to ice cream producers. Add locally-distilled rum to that list of local sweets and the island becomes the stuff of gingermen and rum-cake dreams.

    I rarely drink hot coffee, hot chocolate, or hot toddy in Hawaii as I prefer them iced in warm weather. I know many meld hot chocolate with Christmas memories and, thinking back on this project, I tried to recall the best hot chocolate I ever tasted. Since 1903, *Angelina* on Rue de Rivoli, Paris has poured chocolate so rich it could be mistaken for pudding. Years ago, my friend Emma brought me to *Angelina* while on a short stopover and the experience transformed me. Sadly, I think most Americans would likely consider *Angelina* too fancy for Christmas.

Hot chocolate is not one of my memories from Mom's kitchen; she only mixed up batches from the Swiss Missus. I found a cup near to my heart and not terribly far from my family in Vermont. LA Burdick established his flagship chocolaterie in Walpole, New Hampshire in 1987 and his shops have expanded as far as Chicago and Washington, DC. I often drove to Walpole in fall or winter, either alone or with friends, for a perfectly-baked chocolate madeline and luxurious cup of hot chocolate. In addition to their central New Hampshire location, Burdick's operates a cafe in Harvard Square, which offered succor during long hours of writing my master's thesis and sweetened my Harvard years.

I still wonder if Dad ate any savory pie that Christmas. I hope he did, and perhaps I'm a bit scared to stir that proverbial pudding pot by asking. While it's worth flying to New England for ma Tante Loretta's baking, we now refrain from saying we would "kill" for a piece of her pork pie.

III

Santa Stories

"When I was a kid, I really wanted a metal detector for Christmas, convinced I was going to find buried treasure and could retire at 12. Santa Claus brought me one, but sadly, that treasure was never realized. It's amazing how many bottle caps you have to dig up.
But to be honest, that dream is still alive."
—Peter Billingsley, Ralphie from "A Christmas Carol"

I embraced the jolly to ease my Hawaiian melancholy.

Evidence for the Defense

Dear Editor—
    I am 8 years old. Some of my little friends say there is no Santa Claus. Papa says, "If you see it in The Sun, it's so." Please tell me the truth, is there a Santa Claus?
Virginia O'Hanlon

Virginia, your little friends are wrong. They have been affected by the skepticism of a skeptical age. They do not believe except what they see. They think that nothing can be which is not comprehensible by their little minds. All minds, Virginia, whether they be men's or children's, are little. In this great universe of ours, man is a mere insect, an ant, in his intellect as compared with the boundless world about him, as measured by the intelligence capable of grasping the whole of truth and knowledge.

Yes, Virginia, there is a Santa Claus. He exists as certainly as love and generosity and devotion exist, and you know that they abound and give to your life its highest beauty and joy. Alas! how dreary would be the world if there were no Santa Claus! It would be as dreary as if there were no Virginias. There would be no childlike faith then, no poetry, no romance to make tolerable this existence. We should have no enjoyment, except in sense and sight. The eternal light with which childhood fills the world would be extinguished.

Not believe in Santa Claus! You might as well not believe in fairies. You might get your papa to hire men to watch in all the chimneys on Christmas eve to catch Santa Claus, but even if you did not see Santa Claus coming down, what would that prove? Nobody sees Santa Claus, but that is no sign that there is no Santa Claus. The most real things in the world are those that neither children nor men can see. Did you ever see fairies dancing on the lawn? Of course not, but that's no proof that they are not there. Nobody can conceive or imagine all the wonders there are unseen and unseeable in the world.

You tear apart the baby's rattle and see what makes the noise inside, but there is a veil covering the unseen world which not the strongest man, nor even the united strength of all the strongest men that ever lived could tear apart. Only faith, poetry, love, romance, can push aside that curtain and view and picture the supernal beauty and glory beyond. Is it all real? Ah, Virginia, in all this world there is nothing else real and abiding.

No Santa Claus! Thank God! he lives and lives forever. A thousand years from now, Virginia, nay 10 times 10,000 years from now, he will continue to make glad the heart of childhood.

Francis B. Church
Editor of the *New York Sun*
1897

Those Damn Christmas Shoes

On the big island in the middle of the bigger ocean, the royal poinciana trees, with their flaming flowers set against verdant leaves, lift sullen spirits. The poincianas remind me of their smaller, rosy Mexican friends, the poinsettias. While their nominal stems look similar, the trees from Madagascar were named for a seventeenth-century French governor Mons. Poincy. Diplomats styled the holiday plant for the first US ambassador to Mexico, Joel Roberts Poinsett. In North America, the poinsettia strikes the familiar Christmas image while in the tropics we appreciate the poinciana tree. Like this festive foliage, Christmas cards, songs, and the Hallmark Channel all remind us to go home for the holidays at year's end. I was not going home for the holidays that first year in Hawaii and I continued my search to find both my way and myself on the Big Island.

Our move to the Big Island that summer cost far more than I budgeted. Inflation struck a forty-year high in addition to typically-high island prices. Relocation expenses, which included shipping a car and temporary housing, nearly doubled my budgeted $5,000. When a box of cornflakes at the local supermarket topped $9, I started picking up gig jobs beyond teaching to make ends meet: ride-share driving, photographing foreclosed properties for a bank, cleaning vacation condos, freelance writing, and taking in laundry like Mrs. Cratchit in *A Christmas Carol*.

I read an advertisement from a photography studio seeking a Santa Claus to sit for family Christmas portraits. The idea of revisiting my drama background with its Christmas origins greatly appealed to me; maybe it felt a bit familiar as I acclimated to island life and and the spirited season. When the photography studio offered me an interview, I figured I already had one boot down the chimney given my white hair. I had picked at a few different writing projects, and committed a few thousand uninspired words about trees to my notebook, but my imagination dried like lava in my short island time. *Maybe this Santa stuff will help my creativity?*

I approached the interview seriously and recalled Santas I had known. As a child in Massachusetts, Santa visited our family party every Christmas Eve, with a curled mustache *exactly* like my Uncle Andy. I also saw Santa Claus drive through our small town on his Harley-Davidson—the same motorcycle that looked just like a neighbor's. Regardless of the weather, we routinely saw Santa Claus ringing a bell for the Salvation Army outside the Post Office. Of course, we all knew Mr. Webber dressed as the Post Office Santa, with his white beard unmistakable to the hundreds of teenagers to whom he had taught math. These Santas fit the bill for New England, but the red flannel and cap would scratch me on the Big Island. I decided a convincing Hawaiian Santa needed red board shorts and an aloha shirt, which I could find easily and cheaply.

Like many actors, I did not get the Santa part, and I am not even certain the studio followed through with the project. After reading the news in an email, I walked to my local beach bar,

On The Rocks, to stew. *The Rocks* has everything: surf, sand, sea breeze, thatched roof, an outrigger canoe suspended from the ceiling, muscled surfer bartenders, and unobstructed views of Kailua Bay. Most days I spend a happy hour at *The Rocks*; the bartenders know me and familiar faces abound. I felt sad that Sunday as I sat with my juicy Mai Tais and tried reconciling my new environs with my old memories.

I felt like Stan Zbornak (Herb Edelman), Dorothy's ex-husband from *The Golden Girls*. In December of 1989, Stan arrived at a homeless shelter as an out-of-work and down-on-his-luck Santa. I knew how he felt. I missed plenty of people and the thought of Christmas isolation–even if in paradise–smelled of rotten papayas. The image of Stan in a disheveled Santa suit pushed me to think about my own future. *Why not make the best of this? Why not add to the red shorts and aloha shirt and head out on my own, regardless of the photographer's rejection?* I thought. *I could visit businesses and family parties as a way to make some pocket money for the season.*

Two questions vexed me at the bar: *could I convincingly capture Santa's look, and how much did Santa weigh?* I had 250 pounds stuck in my head, but questioned the number's accuracy. Kona culture favors the ferociously fit; the Iron Man World Championships are held here every fall, so Santa-sized guys remain in the minority, even at *The Rocks*. The bartender, Gunnar–the fittest guy I know–argued Santa weighed in at 320 pounds: "he's got to, that guy is like 6'5."

By text, my sister offered 210 pounds and, as if cued, followed her comment with "But I don't know how male weight works." In the same conversation, my partner Ben said twenty stone (280 lbs).

My good friend, Coach Tim, sardonically wrote "3 bills"

meaning 300 pounds. He quickly followed up with another text: "get off your damn phone and watch the sunset, man."

The authoritative answer, however, came from my friend Kris (of marching band fame). He used to know about big guys.

"340. The Coca-Cola® photo clearly shows a man weighing 340." I considered it the Gospel according to Kris.

In my continued ruminations, I also wondered how one "plays" Santa Claus. Is there a Claus script, or character study, or do we activate memories from youth? Thinking back to the Santas I had known, jollity, size, and facial hair seemed the common factors among them, not entrepreneurial acumen or earnings. Did my profit-driven gig just represent a Scrooge-like sham?

I returned to our condo just a few hundred steps from *The Rocks*. In my closet, I found red high-top Converse® sneakers from a school production of *Grease* several years earlier. *Red sneakers*, I thought. *Yes, a surfin' Santa will need red sneakers and board shorts.* I knew something about putting on a show having produced several large-scale musical productions. I thought I could make surfing Santa a success with my sense of showmanship, but I needed to back up my sense with some financial data. *I hate that damn Christmas shoes song,* I thought as I put the sneakers back.

At my desk, I scribbled numbers on the back of a scrap envelope (the Audubon Society asking for money). I figured less than $200 for supplies, a website, and some graphics design. Print marketing, which I used heavily for other ventures, could prove pricey but it would get my idea into the hands of local business owners. *Could I at least clear $250 to break even and not lose money on the project?* I did not expect to make enough to afford Disney World, but I hoped the project might rekindle some creativity and offset the cost of presents.

I read that by 2022, people moved towards the "gig economy" in greater numbers than ever before. COVID brought about dramatic shifts in the workplace, with whole sectors moving to home-based work and new forms of part-time work. Americans' increasing reliance on home deliveries (from Amazon tchotchkes to food and prescriptions) facilitated by social media platforms and new web technologies fostered significant changes in the economy. The Trump-era virus not only upended the traditional nine-to-five schedule but also offered some additional income as parents stayed home with kids in new, more flexible models of work. In 2014, gig work comprised less than twenty percent of the economy and surpassed thirty-five percent of the economy by 2020, with some 57 million Americans and $1 trillion in goods and services. By 2024, some estimates put gig work at more than half of US wage earners.

I continued scratching the envelope. If I billed at $2 per minute (*Joan Rivers charged $7 per joke just ten years earlier*), I figured I could break even with two to three gigs; anything more counted as sugar. Additionally, if I failed to scrounge up two or three gigs for the season, I needed to rethink the viability of my capitalist project. Even if I flopped I could sell the story you now read and will soon, I hope, review online.

I stared pensively out the kitchen window and saw a moored cruise ship in the bay. In my industrious thinking, did I miss the point of easy island living? In trying to make a buck from Christmas, did I embrace Scrooge before Santa? The prospect of pocketing some extra money and tapping my creativity appealed to me, but the experience did nothing to foster festive feelings. I could not let my Santa venture waste my time, energy, and especially my money. Before making a final decision, I solicited input from people I admired.

Ben sounded skeptical but, as in all things, remained unfailingly supportive. He advocated well for the devil and asked many questions. He agreed that I could play Santa relatively cheap for a bit of fun and a small return on my investment. My aunt Cathy, a longtime and much-admired educator, told me to "go for it" and I had nothing to lose. I appreciated her enthusiasm. I also asked Ma Tante Loretta–my grandmother's sister; at 91 she's a wiz at texting and baking pork pie–who told me I made a great Santa. I appreciated her honesty, which sounds brutal at times.

I needed an expert opinion, so I reached out to a friend with three toddlers. She laughed and asked, "Like a gay daddy Santa? That could have an audience!" Playing *that* kind of Santa escaped my thinking but her suggestion piqued my curiosity. Surely I needed to find some toy soldiers to accompany that act. Ben and I once attended a swanky Palm Springs party with a shirtless Santa sporting a manicured scruff, but I envisioned a wholesome, family fellow for the Big Island. With their endorsements, I ordered the trimmings and initiated my plan.

"If I make a profit," I told Ben after submitting my online order of Santa essentials, "we'll go see *CATS* when the tour wraps in Honolulu in June."

"OK, Tiger," Ben chuckled. "Whatever you purr-fer."

Making a List, Checking it Thrice

The smiling box containing the rest of Big Island Santa's wardrobe arrived in a week. Rather than sweat through the traditional felt suit in Hawaii, I ordered red, knee-length surfboard shorts and a matching aloha shirt festooned with ukuleles and palm trees. I bought size XXL to accommodate my growing costume gut. The wig and beard arrived compressed in a vinyl pouch. I teased them with a brush to animate them. Despite my love of the stage, I had never worn a wig or fake beard and felt uneasy attempting to manipulate the synthetic strands. For all the discussion about drag shows these days, it's a field of show business into which I've not sashayed. Staring into the mirror I saw a portly Brian May with a beard looking contrived and cheesy. My enthusiasm wilted as I arranged my wardrobe, but I still perfunctorily kept all my receipts for my accountant.

To revive my zeal, Ben took me to a secluded beach to take some test photos at dusk. He found a lovely cove lined with palms and shady kiawe trees as well as a deep tide pool, favored by monk seals. If the Swiss Family Robinson came ashore on Hawaii, they would live just as grandly in that cove as they did in New Switzerland. A few people enjoyed that golden hour on the beach and I waited for some to pack up before sheepishly donning the belly, beard, and wig. Ben encouraged me as he suggested different poses and positions, some in the ocean, some on the shore, with both of us fumbling in the tropical twilight to bring about this laughable and long-shot idea. Our relationship reached a new height that afternoon.

Ben treated me to pizza afterward and we scrolled through the photos on my phone. He captured some good shots, including the one on this book's cover. I still saw Brian May washed up on a deserted island but, from a kid's perspective, we thought this Santa might just look the part. I sent what we thought were the best images to my long-time cover designer Anna who worked her magic to enhance the photos for an advertising campaign. In referring to one of the photos, I told Anna, "Please remove the graphic on the leg of my left shorts," to which she replied, "Oh, haha, that's YOU!" At that point, I wondered if I had convincingly stepped into Big Island Santa's red flip-flops.

With the photos captured, I searched for available domain names for the website. Someone had already bought *SeasideSanta, SurfinSanta, SurfingSanta, HawaiiSanta* (as well as *SantaHawaii*), and *BeachbumSanta*. I played with Hawaiian synonyms in my red notebook. *SeashoreSanta* made me think of Sally selling seashells, *PineappleSanta* sounded like something for swingers, and neither *BeachbumClaus* nor *VacationClaus* pleased my ear. But then a beacon appeared, like Rudolph's nose piercing the sky: I found *BigIslandSanta.com* ready to use. I liked it, bought it, and gained a bit of confidence as my "brand" took shape. I built a simple website with a Christmas theme and, within an afternoon, I had put together something that looked legitimate. But when to begin advertising?

I never considered it a simple coincidence that my grandmother named Noella (French for Christmas) loved the yule holiday. Her birthday fell on November 19 and that year she would have turned 89. Launching the website and marketing effort on her birthday seemed a sign, which I considered most auspicious, for all things Christmas. The period between November 19 and December 24 ensured thirty-one days of Big Island Santa, and I liked that it lasted just a month: I could easily envision "thirty-one" like a chocolate Advent calendar.

I gained some unfounded confidence as my micro-gig formed. My parents both made successful entrepreneurs, but I never started my own business nor anticipated what to expect. My only other real self-enterprise—a short-term rental property in Southern California—endured plenty of bumps along the way and repeatedly required adjustments to the project's parameters. During the pandemic, I renovated a 1968 Skyline mobile home. The project could have ended as a financial disaster, although it did not. I lost only the proverbial (and literal) blood, sweat, and tears.

The librarian in me scoured entrepreneurial literature from notable business journals to learn more. The articles all emphasized similar points for aspiring independent contractors: set goals, find your niche with the right clientele, price strategically like Goldilocks (neither too high nor too low), and write a killer pitch. I filled a notebook with ideas; the goals and the pitch came easy, but my notes revealed a struggle to find a niche and strategy. My scribbles included:

Business goals: *Break even, avoid stress, and maybe find a book*
In-demand niche: *Kona = Iron Man triathlon, not a fat man*
Audience: *families with kids + office parties? Gay party Santa?*
Advertising: *mostly Craigslist posts that direct folks to BigIslandSanta.com. Print 40 Santa Xmas cards w/ handwritten notes.*

Pricing: *undercut mainland rates. Beard limitation: like my hair, it's not all white. No beard for me in Hawaii = faux facial hair.* <u>*Keep receipts for deductions.*</u>

Pitch: <u>*Hook someone.*</u>

> *Alo-ho-ho-ho-ha! Does your special wish include sharing Santa's joy with little ones or with your family and friends? Big Island Santa travels to your holiday party at home or on the beach as well as corporate events in offices and restaurants. Big Island Santa is a licensed teacher in Hawaii and has worked with students of all ages and talents for twenty years. Santa helps make your Christmas wish come true. Visit BigIslandSanta.com for more info about Santa and his visits. Mahalo-ho-ho!*

Checking these suggested boxes from the literature, I hoped, would make the Big Island Santa project a success as sweet as a pecan pie.

I published BigIslandSanta.com on November 19 and posted two Craigslist ads. A box of custom Christmas cards arrived that day, and I set to the task of hand writing notes addressed to local business owners. The project started with a fair degree of frustration because only the cards–and not the envelopes–arrived on time. The printer assured the envelopes would arrive by Thanksgiving. More than time, I needed a Santa-size dose of patience to find even a hint of contentment in the project's first week.

Four days passed without a single response to the online ads, and I started sweating like a luau hog. Christmas approached with little time to lose. I turned to my horoscope, a practice only adopted as a Californian: "You may be feeling antsy now,

Gemini, because you cannot predict the outcome of an endeavor you are involved in or one that you are creating," the oracle read. "Try to see the whole thing as a big, fun adventure. That's exactly what it is, and it's part of what makes it valuable." The stars gave me personalized advice and yet, fearing failure, I still wound myself into a stressful panic.

My entrepreneurial optimism waned when four silent days became a week. While unreasonable to expect a response from the mailed cards, I received not as much as a nibble from my online Craigslist ads. Turning again to the stars, I read with great interest on Saturday, November 26: "Sometimes you have to be grateful even for troublesome situations, for they can bring good things, as this one will." These November horoscopes read like fortune cookie wisdom, but the words provided more reassurance that I might reach a greater goal of island contentment, even if I failed at being Santa.

Did my project add to the commercialization of both Santa Claus and Christmas? I heard the voice of Charlie Brown say "good grief," and the Malthusian admonition of Ebeneezer Scrooge that the poor ought to "die and decrease the surplus population." The spreadsheets, written pitches, and postal receipts I collected all suggested contributions to Christmas commercialization, but I had other motivations. A month-long journey lay ahead, and I hardly knew with whom my path might cross during my first December in Hawaii. Journeys, in my experience, always lead to good storytelling, and good storytelling–as I hope you will agree–leads to decent books.

Santa Claus (Finally) Comes to Town

In Hawaii, I appreciate the clerks at Post Office 96740 even more than the elves of the Santa's Village post office in New Hampshire. I especially value them now that I understand the volume of holiday packages shipping to and from the island. In December, a weekday afternoon line at the post office can sink forty-five deep and, at all costs, avoid Saturdays. Imagine my increased annoyance on a Friday afternoon when the line was held-up by–no joke here–a twenty-something surfer mailing three coconuts to the mainland. He did not mail boxed coconuts; no, he shipped fallen-from-the-tree-and-address-the-husk coconuts. Unlike me, the postman remained unfazed. If you doubt me, search "delivering coconuts USPS" and read the article titled *JUST NUTS!*

In my frustration, my phone buzzed and displayed the number for a Hawaii caller. I had two options: answer the call publicly while standing in line, a practice I loathe, or step out of the line and politely answer, knowing that I would lose my spot to no less than the twenty behind me. I chose the latter.

"Aloha," I said.

"Hi, uh aloha, is this Santa, er, Santa's helper?"

"Why yes it is," I replied before eagerly adding a muffled "ho, ho, ho," and stepping farther back.

"This is Sharon. I'm the charge nurse at Leeward Community Hospital. I saw your ad online; I'm hoping you can help us."

"Excellent. What can Santa bring you?"

"Santa usually visits on the Saturday before Christmas so that team members can bring their kids, too. Christmas Eve falls on a Saturday this year and I'm not so sure if we should try that day because we're so under-staffed. It's such a nightmare here."

"Whatever you'd like, Sharon. I'm free on the twenty-fourth or the eighteenth."

"Well, that would be so special on the twenty-fourth, can you really come then? At like three?"

My Happy Hour starts at three.

"Santa never says no," I replied, unsure if I spoke truth.

"OK, good. That's settled. We'll need all the time to prepare. It's such a struggle trying to get nurses on the islands."

"And teachers and doctors, I hear," I said.

"Yes, those, too. OK then, come to the main entrance and the receptionist will tell you where to go. He's very good at giving directions. Send me a message with your fees and things. Mahalo, Santa."

"Mahalo to you," I said as she ended the call.

December twenty-fourth it is.

I tried to rest my mind from Big Island Santa over the weekend. Ben rarely takes time off and I appreciated the opportunity to spend time with him. On Saturday, we walked down to *The Rocks,* to visit our growing bar *'ohana.* The juxtaposition of *The Grinch* broadcast over the bar's television against the crashing surf beyond hit me hard: tropical ocean with a cartoon about a snowy village, coupled with the relative isolation of being "new" in Hawaii with my whole family back east. Although I only invested about $250 into my Big Island Santa venture, I needed to at least break even and take the tax deductions for my expenses and so far I only booked one gig.

On Cyber Monday, November 28–nine days after the launch of BigIslandSanta.com–I received an email from the director of a nearby retirement home: "Aloha Santa," she wrote. "I received your wonderful card in the mail today and I am entertaining the idea of having Santa make a stop at our upcoming employee Christmas Party."

Thank you marketing gods, I thought wearing a Grich-like grin. I composed a brief response outlining Santa's services and encouraged her to reply with any other questions. As the day progressed, I found myself in a bad habit of refreshing my inbox, even though I knew she had likely left for the afternoon. I found her phrase "your wonderful card" energizing, and I hoped that the other thirty-nine business recipients felt similarly. I also reminded myself emphatically: *don't count your Hawaiian snowballs before they melt.* By Wednesday–almost two weeks after my launch–I reached out and she replied with a generous invitation for December 21.

"It's a start," I said aloud to encourage myself.

The two gigs became a significant step towards recovering my money, but they were not enough. I continued to place new advertisements on Craigslist to keep the momentum going. I saw an abundance of Craigslist ads–many duplicates–looking for ride-share drivers (Lyft, Uber) or delivery couriers (Door Dash, Instacart). *They can't deliver better than Santa,* I thought, before I repeated it out loud.

"They can't deliver better than Santa. Damn, that's good," I said to my desk. "In addition to visiting office or home parties,

Santa could deliver locally for you. What better way to send a gift than with Big Island Santa himself?" I posted another ad for my surfin' sleigh service.

Expanding Big Island Santa's menu of offerings surely grew from a place of insecurity and fear of failure. I thought back to my time in Palm Springs–the desert Hollywood for forgotten stars. An iconic statue of Lucille Ball rests on a bench on North Palm Canyon Drive where tourists sit, polish her boob, and snap photos. Yet, Hollywood only considered Lucy a successful actress after the reviews of *I Love Lucy*, and even her drama instructors tried to steer her towards another career. Her legacy and statue now prove her critics wrong. Similarly, the University of Southern California School of Theater, Film and Television denied Stephen Spielberg's admission three times. Only in 2002, after putting the stories of Private Ryan, Oskar Schindler, Indiana Jones, Captain Hook, and E.T. on the big screen did he finish his bachelor's degree. Like Walt Disney, Spielberg knew creative failure too, most notably his flop *1941* from 1979. In December of 1979, Roger Ebert of the *Chicago Sun-Tribune* awarded Spielberg's work just 1.5 stars out of 4 and called the film an "assault on the eyes and ears…that's finally just not very funny."

Think positively, I told myself. *They all made it big, you're only looking to make it small.* As the days turned into weeks and my anxiety increased, I found myself becoming more like Scrooge and less like Santa–whether in line at Starbucks or in Kona town traffic or with the nearby university kids who always seemed to strum their guitars outside of our lanai. The calendar showed us halfway to Christmas and I only had two bookings, which I interpreted as a splendid failure. *So much for CATS,* I told myself. *At least I know how that show ends.*

Look Out Dominic

On December 6, many European children find treats in their shoes left by a bishop in red. Good Saint Nick also looked out for me that day when I received another email addressed to Santa:

> *I just came across your listing on Craigslist and was very happy to see such a unique delivery option...my little sister moved to the Big Island a few months ago to teach 6th graders. My sister's birthday is this Thursday, December 8th. I am looking to have either a cake or cookies delivered to her at the school during lunchtime at 11:45.*

I recommended my favorite island baker and the client made the arrangements from Connecticut. Despite the smallness of the gig, just $15, I felt my efforts had gained some attention. When he made his advanced payment, he generously sent $20. I made myself available from 11-12 on Thursday and, with careful planning, assured success for Big Island Santa's delivery debut. With Hawaii's minimum wage at $12 per hour, I estimated I hit the earnings ballpark by including mileage and tip.

After St. Nick's Day on December 6, some celebrate December

8 as a holy day marking Mary's Immaculate Conception, that is, *Mary's* conception without sin by her parents, Joachim and Anne. Some Christians also celebrate the "Annunciation" nine months before Christmas on March 25 when Mary became "with child." As for Christmas, the best interpretations calculate a spring birth, not a day counted among the solstice festivities.

I had errands in town that morning before making Santa's special delivery. I felt a bit nervous but tried to channel the anxiety into enthusiasm by wearing a red-and-white baseball shirt and red shorts in anticipation of Santa's opening act.

I walked past St. Michael's Church and its lush green lawn. Near the neighbors' plastic Nativity stands a lovely Marian grotto built of coral and lava stones. A parish priest built the grotto in 1940 and only the shrine remains from the original church, which was rendered unsafe from a 2006 earthquake. Remembering the old hymn to Mary eased my nerves that morning: *"Immaculate Mary, your praises we sing; you reign now in splendor with Jesus our king."* I smiled and thought, *with Mary on my side, what can go wrong?*

Before changing into my costume, I collected the cake without fuss from the handsome young baker (I said he was my favorite). He reminded me with wide eyes: "Hold the box bottom or it'll fall through." I appreciated his admonition as I easily envisioned Big Island Santa dropping the lovely Chantilly cake on the school's curb. I only had to drive fifteen minutes from the bakery to the school. Satisfied with the precision of my timing, my little car climbed from the seashore town up to the hillside school. I stopped to add my belly, red sneakers, and shirt; leaving the wig and beard for the final moment. I looked to my left to see the expansive ocean beyond the hardened lava fields. *This is such a weird idea you've had,* I told myself before I parked and phoned the school office and spoke with the secretary.

"Hi. I'm here with a birthday cake for Ms. Adhikari. Sixth grade."

"You're supposed to bring it to her workplace?" the secretary interrogated. The teacher in me knew this seasoned secretary kept order in that office.

"Yes. Her family gave me those instructions from Connecticut," I said. "Also, I'm dressed as Santa. I don't want to alarm anyone."

"Oh. Okay. Hold please," she said.

I waited less than a minute.

"Yeah, hi, Ms. Adhikari is not on campus today," the woman said when she returned.

"Really? Are you sure?" I asked.

"Yes, I'm looking at the absence list now...Santa."

"Okay, thank you then," I said before hanging up.

My plan failed to anticipate Ms. Adhikari's absence. I called her brother in Connecticut for instructions.

"Hi sir," I said. "I'm so sorry to bother you, but it seems that your sister isn't at school today."

"Really?" he said.

"The secretary just said she wasn't on campus."

"Let me call her and see where she's at."

"No problem," I replied. "I'll wait to hear from you."

I sat in my car and watched the school yard. A bell rang at 11:45 and students milled about; many headed for the open-door cafeteria. The client called back.

"I'm really sorry. She took the day off for her birthday," he told me. "She went to see that erupting volcano. I guess it's not close. She said to leave the cake at the school and she'll share it on Monday."

"Yes; that volcano is well south of here. No problem, I'll leave it with the office secretary for her."

"Thank you so much, Santa, you've been great. What a fantastic service you offer."

"My pleasure," I said.

I took off my belly before walking into the office, leaving it with the beard and wig, as I carried the thick cake to the office. Both the number and size of middle schoolers walking about made the place feel more like a high school.

Students swarmed in the office to buy tickets for their "Snow Ball" dance; the idea still makes me laugh. I saw an adult standing toward the rear of the room and I walked straight towards her. She looked more like a vice principal than a school secretary and she greeted me with a big smile.

"Hi, I just called, I have this birthday cake to deliver for Ms. Adhikari, but I hear she's out today. Her brother said to leave it with you until she returns."

"Oh, that's a lovely cake," the woman said with a wry smile. "What a shame for her to be sick on her birthday."

Yeah, sick, I thought, stifling a Grinchy smile.

As I returned to my car, I wanted someone to care similarly for my sister while I lived so far away. I hoped my service would provide some light on gloomy Christmases, but unease continued to gnaw inside of me. Sitting in the school parking lot, I scribbled a note: *This is dumb. Really dumb. I'm trying too hard to like Hawaii,* before driving towards *The Rocks* to numb myself with a pirate-sized pour of Gunnar's rum.

On Saturday, I listened from the lanai as the December rain slowed to a pitter-patter while Ben recuperated from the flu in bed. The weather either drowned out the student singers next door or just kept them inside, and I considered the daytime quiet an early Christmas present. My phone buzzed on the nearby desk and displayed the contact information for nurse Sharon at the hospital. *She must be calling to confirm.*

"Alo-ho-ho-ho-ha," I said, adding in a little character work.

"Hi Santa, it's Sharon from the hospital." She sounded sullen.

"I'm looking forward to visiting you and your team, Sharon."

"Oh, that's just it, Santa. I'm calling to cancel."

"But you can't cancel Christmas, only I can do that." I tried to raise her spirits.

"We just don't have the staff to allow for anything fun. We're a skeleton crew for Christmas Eve. It's horrible."

"Then you need Santa to come and cheer you up, Sharon. Would another day be better or another time?"

"I thought about that. There just isn't a good time. I feel awful because I know it would bring some joy to the hospital but we're stretched so thin that I'm trying to minimize distractions and interruptions to our workflow. I'm really, really sorry, Santa."

"Well, I trust your judgment, Sharon. If you change your mind, you have my number; please don't hesitate to call. I do hope you can have a Merry Christmas."

"You, too, Santa. You, too."

I switched off my phone and sat on the lanai as the rain fell. Then I heard a discordant noise, just as I shut my eyes to compose myself. I heard "Hark! The Herald Angels Sing" poorly strummed on a guitar by a student on their campus.

It could be worse, I told myself. *It could be a ukulele.*

Grandma Got...

Thankfully, Big Island Santa avoided Ben's illness as the remaining visits of the season approached: first, at a nearby retirement home on December 21, and second, a delivery the following day to a doctor's office. For the retirement home, I gathered my costume parts and left the condo complex in plain clothes. Superman–with his washboard abs–had an easier costume change than Santa as I tried to "become" the Claus in an empty parking lot ("Island Dialysis") nearby. Also, Superman kept his face clean-shaven and his hair pasted with Brylcreem. I looked in the rear view mirror and practiced a "ho, ho, ho" one last time before stepping out of the car as Big Island Santa.

I walked up the nursing home's driveway recalling my Disney World lesson with Peter Pan: he never broke character and he talked in Peter's quick manner. Peter took his time and said something special to everyone who had waited to see him; the skill came in making the visitor feel special with unbroken eye contact. *Easy peasy*, I told myself.

My big Santa belly rumbled with butterflies as sweat dripped down my back, both beard and wig itched with my fast-rising body temperature. An elderly gentleman with cotton-puff eyebrows greeted me at the reception desk. I wondered if he lived or worked there.

"Welcome Santa," he said with a grin. "The party is that way," and he pointed across the lobby.

"Why thank you, young man," unsure if the response sounded funny or saccharine.

I walked across the lobby with its typical durable furniture. I could see a small group of people gathered just beyond with a buffet table laden with food, but not many children. I had no time to delay. *This is it. I'm Santa.*

"Alo-ho-ho-ho-ha!" I bellowed as some turned to look.

Perhaps I expected a little more celebrity status than reasonable, although one dad found me hilarious and laughed every time he passed by. The little kids stood apprehensively but enjoyed the handfuls of candy that came out of Santa's bag. I remembered my lesson with Peter Pan and got down on a knee to look the tots in their eyes. The teens appeared more fun in their skepticism and their surprise when Santa asked about their progress in geometry. I found chit chat with the parents difficult, but I seemed to keep the kids' attention. Two teens sang an impromptu rendition of "Jingle Bells" for me, to which I overwhelmingly cheered and mulled the idea of adding Karaoke Santa the following year. The host generously invited me to share in their luau but, alas, to keep his beard white, Santa never eats on duty–minus fireside cookies, of course.

After making the rounds to the tables of feasters and posing for pictures with the youngest, we played games, shared laughs, and they exchanged gifts. As a teacher, I evaluate performances and gave myself a solid (and likely generous) "B" for an above-average performance. The experience felt different than envisioned, but did that difference stem from the Hawaiian experience of Christmas or just my amateur performance?

The sun dipped below the ocean horizon on the shortest day of the year as Big Island Santa left the nursing home waving to some unsuspecting residents. I missed an opportunity to visit with them and wonder now if the man in red works better as a resource to area charities instead of my entrepreneurial venture. Despite the warm weather, I considered the afternoon a tepid success as the last of the sun's setting rays kissed my face, although I think I preferred Jack Frost's nip on the nose.

Big Island Santa made another special delivery on December 22, more successfully than at the middle school. I had to collect a large platter of sushi rolls for a doctor's office in town. All went smoothly, and the women of the office laughed with great frivolity at the novelty of a speedy-delivery Santa. We posed for pictures, Santa asked if they had all been nice (the aides said they had but not the naughty doctor), I handed out some candy, and, as Santa's style, vanished like a puff of smoke.

I chose December 23 as the last day I checked Big Island

Santa's email inbox and removed the last of the Craigslist advertisements. With no more bookings, the time arrived for Ben and me to enjoy the holidays. In the new year, I would examine the Big Island Santa project and assess whether or not to try again. For the present, we turned to Christmas Eve merriment and I tried to bury the frustration of my canceled hospital appearance.

Let the Jingle Bells Rock

"Should I just go and surprise the hospital staff as Santa?" I asked when we returned from our volcano trek.

"Well, you don't want to add to what sounds like a very stressful holiday. Let's just enjoy a quiet Christmas Eve together. Let's start with a drink at *The Rocks.*"

The Christmas Eve hula dancer wore a flaming poinciana dress, matching the crimson of the setting sun. Other than her festive dress, and a few extra Christmas tunes played on the ukulele, the familiar *Rocks* vibe felt the same as any other night.

"Merry Christmas, guys. The usual?" Gunnar asked.

"No, my good man," I said. "I think I'll change it up tonight."

Gunnar paused his reach for a rocks glass.

"Instead of rum and Coke tonight," I started, "I'll go for Coke and rum."

He laughed while Ben rolled his eyes.

"Long Board for me, please," said Ben, turning to me and leaving Gunnar to his art. "You know, perhaps Santa should slow down on the sauce in the new year."

"You're not wrong, Ben."

"I'm not saying you're in trouble," Ben interrupted. "A dry January is good for us all."

"No promises I'll go dry, but cutting back is a good idea.

Thanks for looking after me." I kissed Ben on the cheek as the bartender brought our drinks. "What's Santa bringing you tonight, Gunnar?"

"Cash, I hope," said the young Gen-Z instantly. "And maybe sneakers from my dad."

His innocent answer reminded us that, at twenty-four, Gunnar was the same age as my sister.

"Here's to a Merry Christmas," Ben said, raising his glass as we toasted our bartender.

We enjoyed a pleasant evening at *The Rocks*, but that Christmas Eve lacked the enchantment of those in my childhood. I had grown up and moved far from snowy New England and our traditional Christmases. Despite that distance, Ben created a festive meal at home with a fresh fish filet and golden potatoes. I sliced into a pineapple rum cake for dessert. Although not the rambunctious gathering we knew as children, our Hawaiian Christmas felt homelike, and we had cleaned the condo before 8:00.

"Do you want to go back to *The Rocks*?" I asked Ben.

"Yeah, we might as well. Gunnar stays open until 9. Or 9:30 for us."

Again we strolled to the shore and some who had remained at the bar applauded us on our return. We weren't looking for a boozy Christmas, but to spend time together and oceanside. Sitting at a beach bar on Christmas Eve remains a foreign idea in my family but, in this instance, especially considering the seaside location, I could envision worse ways to spend the evening, and it surely uplifted my spirit.

I enjoyed a chilled glass of pinot along the shore's edge and remembered how blessed I was to spend the holidays with Ben, as well as to be in electronically close contact with faraway family and friends. There are lots of lonely people during the holidays; indeed, I had experienced loneliness myself during earlier Christmases. Depression, substance abuse, and terminal illness all represent real-world hardships that persist on December 25; in fact, those hardships often exacerbate during the last week of the year. Who recalls the true holiday horrors of a cooked turkey flying off the table and out an open window, or other gatherings that ended in tears of gin? Such trauma exists at the heart of classic Christmas stories like *Christmas Vacation* and *A Christmas Story*, and we call them "classic." In the future, perhaps Big Island Santa should look out for those found on the margins of life rather than worry about booking corporate parties. My mother and grandmothers would agree with that.

Few towns dress themselves up for Christmas like Disney World which, I imagine, stems from the fact that few "towns" calculate a *per capita* revenue stream like Disney World. From their theme parks to their cruise ships to their entertainment products and merchandise, The Walt Disney Company surely knows how to make money every season, but old Walt himself knew lean times, too. A newspaper editor reportedly fired him for lacking imagination and a number of his early businesses ended in bankruptcy. With persistence, his brand certainly exploded over the last century. I didn't expect Big Island Santa to debut like the Mouse, but Disney's example reminded me to continue in the face of festive frustration.

Had I commercialized Christmas like a movie or a theme park? Well, Scrooge (or at least Dickens) grew better for it. Ebeneezer didn't give all his money to the poor like a mendicant; he used his money to enrich the lives of others. Dickens himself wrote for money, not art. Let's return one last time to Scrooge:

"It was always said of him that he knew how to keep Christmas well, if any man alive possessed the knowledge. May that be truly said of us, and all of us!" As we approach the bicentennial of the story's publication, I still wonder how we keep Christmas today.

We still play "Do They Know It's Christmas" and we still collect for charity in a world where problems seem to get bigger, not smaller, and the rich continue to get richer. Although the Scrooges among us often give in order to reap the tax benefits, if their charity improves someone's living, then complaints may be misplaced. I also think an impulse persists to gather with friends and family as well as exchange good wishes as much as Scrooge's nephew Fred invited him for the holiday. I hope the desire, among families like the Cratchits and mine, to take whatever we have and make it special, continues for generations, but I wonder how practical that sentiment remains as many of us keep moving farther afield.

Now that I'm in my forties, I'm the same age as my grandmothers when I toddled about. In this little book, I've remembered the food, trimmings, and presents through which they, and my mom, made Christmas so special, but I wonder if they were content with all that festive work. In hindsight, it looks truly exhausting. Yet, if I step into their shoes, I want to believe they found contentment, year after year, in giving to family and friends. It's a different experience for us on the island: our bellies are full, we are blessed with a comfortable home, good friends, and we are loved–even if from a distance—but it looks quite dissimilar to my childhood experience.

Perhaps it's not a feeling to reserve for December 25 but instead a year-round awareness, and a feeling to sustain us through the melancholic months. Scrooge had all the money he needed, but once upon a time he kept his counting chambers and townhouse cold and dark. Only in sharing did the old man find joy. In that 1989 Christmas episode of *The Golden Girls*, Stan Zbornak got over himself and turned his misery into merriment, much like the Grinch, Charlie Brown, George Bailey, and I think even me.

As my Christmas story draws to a close, where do you think the savvy librarian should catalog and shelve this little book? Yes, *Big Island Santa* fits into the capitalist critiques like *A Christmas Carol*, *It's A Wonderful Life*, and *White Christmas*. Make no mistake, my childhood Christmases looked like those historical docudramas of Chevy Chase's *Christmas Vacation* and Ralphie's *Christmas Story*. I'd also like to think our not-so-subtle love story could be yet another *Love Actually* rom-com vignette. Lastly, I'll testify in court that Joan Webber's Nativity pageants were greater than *The Greatest Story Ever Told*. There's no shortage of library shelves onto which librarians could stash these 25,000 words. This librarian suggests cataloging it at PS648.C45 (American Literature / Prose / Christmas stories) after story topics such as the Amish, baseball, California, "Chick Lit" (PS648.C415), and just before stories about dragons. I also wouldn't mind sitting beside Dolly's *Little Whorehouse* if given a choice.

America is no longer that which Norman Rockwell illustrated. America today is blessedly diverse and continues to bring together many languages and customs as Lady Liberty promises. So, too, have Christmases changed for my family, especially my mother. It's no doubt hard for her to have family spread as far as it is, but she and Dad continue to find their puppyless way.

After 200 years, the terrors shown to Scrooge by the Christmas wraiths remain as relevant as ever, not only for Big Island

Santa, but perhaps for all of us with a bit more to share. We're told to believe that the Christ child, though swaddled from the cold night air, radiated warmth in the simplicity of his family's love. I remember that image in Mrs. Webber's fabulous fifteen-minute Christmas pageant and the many other Christmas snapshots Mom sent to me through the mail. I certainly had the benefit of knowing that peace with my family in Christmases past, in my own Christmas isolation at times, and with Ben at Christmas present. Finding that inner peace, either for a converted Scrooge or a shepherd under a cold, starry sky, is what Big Island Santa might have sought in that photographer's job. Hopefully, I passed a little of that contentment onward, whether or not dressed in Santa's aloha red. I wish that same peace and contentment for you.

Our decorative Charlie Brown tree branch drooped low on that Hawaiian Christmas morning. I know that's the point of a Charlie Brown tree, but it nudged me to think about something a bit better for the next year. We enjoyed a breakfast of pineapple rum cake, warm biscuits, and coffee while listening to Art Lyman's 1964 *Mele Kalikimaka* album. We tore open our presents like little kids, but there weren't any surprises: books, booze, a summer sausage for Ben, and some other silly things. We celebrated a modest Christmas, but one in which we felt loved and grateful for our restful time together. Text messages from mainland friends arrived overnight like presents from Santa, and we pored over the pictures, gifs, and memes that marked our twenty-first-century techno-holiday.

* * *

"Did you empty your stocking, Peter Pan?" Ben asked.

"I think so, but let me check." I shook the green sock and its bell jingled. The felt stocking measured larger, but lighter, than those Mémère Aubuchon knitted for us and I missed hers, although I know Mom safeguards it in Vermont. As I reached into the toe and withdrew a small envelope, which read *Big Island Santa* in red script.

"Looks like it's for you, Santa."

I opened it and found two tickets to see *CATS* in Honolulu, but no note.

"I guess we're going to see *CATS*," I told Ben, although I think he already knew as much. "This will be my seventh time seeing it on stage."

"If you see it nine times, maybe something magical happens like you're reborn."

"Remember our first Christmas in 2019, when I had just moved to California? The *CATS* movie played in theaters then and we went to see it."

"If I recall, we went to see it and then God punished the whole world with the scourge of COVID. You should take the hint."

"Stop," I said, laughing. "That's a great Christmastime memory."

"I'm hoping the show is better than the movie," he said.

I told Siri to play a jellicle jingle. She didn't understand my request and gave me "Jingle Bells" instead, which was just as good for that Hawaiian holiday.

Epilogue

A Bright Hawaiian New Year's Day

We traveled to Honolulu to celebrate the new year with throngs of revelers. The city retained more lingering Christmas decorations than the Big Island, but these looked unlike those from my New England memories. In my head, I heard Bing Crosby's dulcet "Silver Bells" with its mention of "Strings of street lights / Even stop lights / Blink a bright red and green," as we headed to the city's hot new "tiki" bar: *Skull & Crown Trading Co.*

Jasper, a very fit firefighter moonlighting as a ride-share driver, picked us up not once but twice that evening and he regaled us with stories of his fireman's pole. He calls HFD Station No. 1 in Chinatown his home base, and he knows well the *Skull and Crown's* neighborhood. In the 1800s, Honolulu's Chinatown stood as an unplanned amalgamation of dilapidated wooden structures with outdoor toilets and cesspools alongside livestock pens and chicken coops breeding abundant rats, maggots, lice, flies, and cockroaches. The city imposed new building codes after a late-century fire consumed eight blocks of the wooden warren and displaced the residents of more than 7,000 homes, but few builders paid attention to these codes during Chinatown's reconstruction.

Within a decade, city officials quarantined a Chinatown outbreak of bubonic plague by setting some forty-one controlled fires in the neighborhood. On January 20, 1900, Board of Health workers lit a sanitizing fire at the corner of Beretania and Nuuanu streets, which quickly spread to the wooden Kaumakapili Church nearby and eventually reached the wharf, consuming thirty-eight acres and 4,000 homes over seventeen days. Today's Chinatown buildings, including the *Skull and Crown*, are of brick construction because the threat of fire persisted well into the twentieth century.

From the outside, the *Skull & Crown* looks like another century-old brick storefront or barbershop; stepping into the historic watering hole returns you to the early 1900s. If you've not read our other fifty-two reviews of Pacific "tiki" bars, do get yourself a copy of **Ben & Jeff's Pacific Adventure: Pursuing the Perfect Mai Tai**—it's Santa's gift of choice.

SKULL & CROWN TRADING Co. / 2 N Hotel St, Honolulu, Hawaii / full menu. *Not only the best Pacific Pop bar in Honolulu, but the best of the archipelago.* When to go: 5 to 11 Tues-Sat. Closed Sunday/Monday.

Atmosphere (5): The sole tiki artifact inside *Skull & Crown*, an eight-foot carved ki'i of the war god Ku, watches revelers from the corner. The many other well-chosen artifacts create a PacPop paradise, fusing Asian and Oceanic items from brass Chinese dragons to a vintage scuba helmet with a moose head hung on the brick wall near a reclining mermaid. The decor recalls our other favorite, San Diego's *Grass Skirt*, but *Skull & Crown* presents the beachcomber style without cultural appropriation.

Mai Tai (5): The barkeep mixes a perfect 1944 original. You can't miss *S&C's* Mai Tai, but with so many other unique offerings to sample, try their other crafts, too.

"We'll be there before long," Ben said as we passed the Blaisdell Center with banners announcing the spring run of CATS. "By then, we'll be halfway to next Christmas."
   I smiled at the thought.

Apart from the 44,000 residents of America Samoa, the fireworks over Waikiki Beach represent the last major U.S. city to ring in the new year, and it's a fun place to be, especially in your bathing shorts and tank-top at midnight–it sure makes the folks in Times Square look, well, cold.

Bussing to New Year's celebrations, Honolulu, 2022

I considered Big Island Santa's return in the new year. As it usually takes an abundance of resources to energize even a small side hustle, I looked back at the November goals in my notebook before making any new resolutions: *Break even, don't stress, and maybe find a book in the experience.* I failed to break even but my losses amounted to less than $75. I knew reporting a business loss had tax advantages, so although I hadn't met the goal, I also didn't fall too short. As for stress, well, I had stressed, and not just about Big Island Santa. Achieving a better sense of contentment needed to be a life commitment in Hawaii, not just a business goal. I suppose my journey as Big Island Santa was, in many ways, a journey towards understanding both contentment and joy.

* * *

I completed the final edits to this project in Kathmandu, not Kona, when school was in recess for Nepal's principal festival: Dashain. We're in the midst of fifteen days of celebration marking the triumph of the powerful Hindu goddess Durga over evil. Children fly kites and swing on specially-constructed bamboo *"linge pings"* while feasting and illuminated decorations stretch across all fifteen days. Although I understand very little of the sights and sounds around me, the love between family and friends is beginning to look a lot like Christmas. I'm glad to know that, as much as customs vary from Nepal to London and from New England to the Big Island, there's a universal impulse to share seasonal joy. How blessed I am to start to understand as much.

Lastly, let me acknowledge and thank Benjamin Tautges for his developmental editing, critique, and proofreading of this manuscript, 143 times.

Kathmandu, October 2024

Afterword

On a Thursday evening in early January 2023, the combination of winter clouds and volcanic mist fused to create the most spectacular bayside sunset I ever saw. How do you describe the color when it includes every imaginable hue of crimson? The inflamed sky burned pink with the flamboyance of a plastic flamingo and the extravagance of an archbishop's scarlet cassock. Or perhaps the royal poincianas washed the skyline with their red to match Big Island Santa's shorts.

That sunset burned at the start of my first rehearsal with the Kona Choral Society. My new year began with a new group of a hundred friends surrounding me. While we did not sing "He shall reign forever" as they had during the blustery *Messiah* afternoon a month before, we practiced a robust Gospel number–perfectly written for the range of my *profundo* voice–aptly called "The Storm Is Passing Over." So it seemed.

Christmas turned to Lent and Lent became Holy Week. *"When April with his showers sweet with fruit,"* wrote Chaucer, *"The drought of March has pierced unto the root."* Tax season bloomed.

"My accountant is calling to discuss my tax returns today," I told Ben over our morning coffee. "She says I'm getting a sizable refund."

"Excellent. I think you should spend it at Disneyland Paris this summer," Ben replied.

"Really? That's such a splurge."

"Yes, but you seemed more peaceful after you saw your friends. I think it's a good investment."

"Wow, *CATS* and Disneyland Paris, what a summer," I said jokingly. "Maybe I will."

My accountant runs an efficient meeting. My refund easily covered a weekend trip to Paris, and that pleased me. Just at the end of the meeting, however, she made one disappointing comment.

"This Big Island Santa thing is a hobby, not a business, by IRS standards," she told me.

"Hobby expenses are taxable?" I asked, anticipating her answer.

"For the IRS, a business makes a profit, made a profit previously, or will likely make a profit, depending on the income from the activity. Claiming a hobby as a business could trigger an audit."

"OK," I said. "Understood. But how does the IRS feel about the Easter Bunny?"

A Holiday Game

As I wrote my Big Island Santa experience, the book grew to include even more holiday memories, helping me contextualize the story. I hope I have similarly mixed nostalgia with observation for you, but if not, here is a list of twenty-five questions to bake your own holiday memories.

You can use this list in many different ways: for your own reflection, or as journal prompts, or as a round-the-table discussion starter at a holiday meal. If you play a "Yankee Swap" or "White Elephant" gift exchange game, consider matching the question numbers below to recipients of prizes (before they can choose a prize, they must answer the question with the corresponding number). You might consider just one question a day as Christmas nears, or use them all at once at a holiday party. Surely the responses will be less guarded if answers accompany a responsible sip of mulled wine or hot toddy. For all responses, make sure you explain why.

1. Did you ever kiss Santa Claus?
2. What is your favorite holiday food?
3. How big do you like your snowballs?
4. Who was your favorite mistletoe kiss?
5. What's the best TV Christmas special?
6. Which is your favorite Christmas film?
7. What is your least favorite holiday food?

8. Was *Die Hard* (1988) a Christmas movie?
9. What's printed on a good Christmas card?
10. Are Christmas theme parks cool or creepy?
11. What is the best thing to do with fruitcake?
12. Who made Christmas most special for you?
13. What are your favorite Christmas heirlooms?
14. What was the best Christmas you spent away?
15. What was your naughtiest Christmas moment?
16. Who is the Scrooge of your life? Can he change?
17. If Christmas was canceled, where would you go?
18. Which part would you choose to play in a pageant?
19. What was the best Christmas gift you ever received?
20. Is Rudolph's dentist friend Herney gay or confused?
21. What was the worst Christmas gift you ever received?
22. What are three places where NOT to put a candy cane?
23. What's your favorite Christmas song (carol or popular)?
24. Did you have 'James Stewart' or 'Chevy Chase' at home?
25. Santa Claus: a real guy or really bad lie? Can you prove it?

Postscript

The story of Big Island Santa sat untouched for two years. Perhaps feeling a bit of nostalgia, I picked it up again as a Peace Corps Response Volunteer in Nepal. After just three months of site work, I chose to hastily return to Massachusetts for my grandfather's funeral: a twenty-four hour journey to Leominster by plane, train, and automobile (the eponymous movie is about Thanksgiving, not Christmas). At 92, no death is unexpected, but my grandfather's decline advanced faster than we imagined. I am sure he planned it that way as the guy never overstayed a welcome, a trait I describe in *Flocked* (2022).

I last spoke to him on his birthday as he turned 92. That was the rare day when fresh air blew the clouds away to unmask some snow-capped peaks of the Himalayas–a sight I can see from my front door. I remember describing them to my grandfather on the phone and his response sounded similar to any of his responses to his grandkids' adventures: "isn't that something?" For my family, Christmas will feel different this year as his absence will be especially noticed; but, perhaps therein lies the reason for this little collection of yuletide memories: as much as we think Christmas traditions stay the same, they are also inescapably different every year. Whatever the circumstance of your holiday as you read this, I wish you abundant peace from the foothills of Nepal.

A "Flocked" Feature

My Grandparents, Midcentury America & Plastic Flamingos

In 2022, I published *Flocked* as a 90th birthday gift for my grandfather. He told me he liked it in his own, quiet way, which was the only review I needed. With his recent passing at 92, we remembered a life that spanned the twentieth and twenty-first centuries: as an Atomic Veteran who witnessed nuclear explosions in the South Pacific, to a post-war family man, homeowner, and pioneering plastics industrialist that unfailingly served his family, church, and community.

In 1955, the year after Paramount released *White Christmas*, he bought the house at 8 June Street, just a mile from where he was born. He used all $5,000 of his GI benefits, "but I never had a mortgage," he always said, before insisting, "I bet I can get double for it now." He lived there for seventy years and, after a decline that did not last two weeks, he moved on from that same house to meet my grandmother at long last.

I think highly of my grandfather, and while *Flocked* touches on some often-praiseworthy family history, the book tells the bigger story of the city's role in plastics manufacturing. Not long after his passing, I read that the Tupperware Company (which began in Leominster) had filed for bankruptcy, truly marking the end of an era in plastics manufacturing. A sample from Part 2 of *Flocked* follows.

America at the Midcentury

New roadside attractions and destinations like Disneyland–cultivated from orange groves in Anaheim, California–also emerged with the infrastructure provided by the Interstate System. The theme park opened on July 17, 1955 and forever changed Americans' relationship between leisure and consumer culture. On the East Coast, Interstate 95 connected New England with Florida, sending northern "snowbirds" south during the cold winters. The Interstate also expedited the delivery of consumer goods, now further popularized by television advertisement. In addition to Tupperware, homemakers named appliances such as the Sunbeam electric frypan, a Tappan microwave oven, or the Kenmore 12-speed mixer as time-saving must-haves for the kitchen. In the laundry room, new top-loading washers and front-loading dryers supposedly made the homemaker's work easier and more efficient. The big shipping trucks also brought Howdy Doody and Barbie dolls, Superman lunch boxes, and copies of *Mad Magazine* (my dad's favorite) for the kids from coast to coast. A grill and backyard furniture could ship to any backyard kingdom. Shipping consumer goods and plastic wares became easier when construction finished for Interstate routes such as I-190, which intersects with Leominster's Lancaster Street, where the plastic factories stood.

Leominster saw the birth of the biggest names in plastics technology like DuPont, Foster Grant, and Tupperware as well as Borden Chemicals and others. Central to this story is another smaller shop that distributed its wares coast to coast. Founded in 1946 by James Sullivan and George Progin on Leominster's Union Street, Union Products' office and factory eventually moved to Lancaster Street with their competitors. Yet unlike Foster Grant's sunglasses, DuPont's chemicals, or Tupper's home wares, Union Products carved a niche for themselves in exterior plastic decorations. From their modest beginnings, they grew into a 100-strong team and produced memorable holiday characters for home trimming and illumination.

My grandfather went to work at Union Products when he returned from military service in 1955. According to him, "Things got real slow at that time, so I brought in my package of lawn ornaments." These were the same lawn ornaments he carved from wood in the garage on Sixth Street while sipping Moxie. "They ended up making a lot of the things I had," including a carved flamingo. The original product took the shape of a flat plastic cutout, just like the earlier combs cut from celluloid. The first flamingos from Union Products barely resembled the one known today. In 1956, the company hired art-school-graduate Don Featherstone to improve the look, feel, and dimension of the lawn ornaments. Featherstone reportedly studied images from an issue of *National Geographic Magazine* ("Ballerinas in Pink") and molded the three-dimensional version that has become the Lord of Lawns. The flamingo, however, was not Featherstone's first project; he molded a plastic dog and a duck before starting on the pink project. In fact, according to Featherstone in 1998, the duck sold better up to that point than the flamingo. Yet, of all of Union Products' products, it's the flamingo that endures more than any other on landscaped lawns and in popular culture.

Production for Union Products' flamingos began in time for the birds to be included in the Sears 1957 Spring/Summer catalog under the heading: "Weather-Resistant Plastic Lawn Displays." The advertisement continued to lure buyers by encouraging them to, "Add a distinctive touch to your home" with "sparkling, gleaming colors, so easy to set up," with ad copy that read like Tupper's. A pair of Union Products' flamingos sold for $2.76 a pair while Featherstone's other duck design of a "Snow white mother and three ducklings" sold for $2.68. In addition to Sears, which carried the birds in their catalog until 1970, flamingos retailed at Woolworth's and similar stores. In the decades that followed, the flamingos found great popularity in diverse neighborhoods across the country. At Union Products, however, the flamingo was just one of 800 other lawn ornaments made for spring, summer, Halloween, and Christmas designed as part of the consumer manufacturing cycle in which goods are designed, produced, sold, and then retired when fallen out of fashion. As neighboring manufacturers closed their doors in the 1980s and '90s, Union Products–then under Featherstone's leadership–continued production until the summer of 2006 when it sold the 20 millionth flamingo and closed the shop doors citing, among other things, skyrocketing utility costs.

As Ronald Modra and Mary Beth Roberts illustrated in *Garish Gardens, Outlandish Lawns*, it's not just the flamingos or the plastic Union Products' ornaments that have captured the imagination of Americans: there's a whole lawn-decorating culture that graces Eisenhower's highways and rural byways as well as revolutionized the auto culture that followed. The plastic flamingo provided an easy escape from the boring backyard to more exotic climates–or, at least, Florida. There's irony in the association of Florida with the pink birds; as Jennifer Price points out, settlers there hunted flamingos to extinction in the late-nineteenth century for both their feathers and their meat.

They call Featherstone "The Flamingo King" but Modra and Roberts' late-1990s road trip highlighted many other enduring displays made from inexpensive materials: from two-dimensional wood cutouts of bashful boys and whirling roadrunner windmills like those my grandfather carved as a boy to gregarious garden gnomes, discarded toilets that serve as petunia planters, and all manner of mailboxes. They also cite Mary-Elizabeth Buckham of Centreville, Maryland and her flock of thirty-four plastic flamingos that she dresses and arranges in tableaux, like a Christmas manger scene. Lawn displays might not be your cup of tea, but it's midcentury Americana that speaks to domestic brands, highway culture, and plastics that altered the American landscape after the flamingo hatched in 1957.

*Flocked: **My Grandparents, Midcentury America & Plastic Flamingos** (2022) is published by 92252 Press and available from online booksellers like Amazon. ISBN: 978-1734059274

About the Author

Jeffrey W. Aubuchon debuted as a shepherd in Joan Webber's 1987 Nativity pageant, with costume sewn by his mother and shepherd's crook carved by his grandfather. He later played the Third King, Joseph, and, in his sixth year, the Announcing Angel. As a Peace Corps Volunteer, he first lived among the shepherds of southern Morocco and, twenty years later, with the farmers of central Nepal. After honing his writing and singing skills at Saint Anselm College and Harvard University, he directed hundreds of students on stage in more than a dozen productions. When stateside, he resides in Hawaii.

Read more at **jeffreywaubuchon.com** and follow him on social platforms.

Also by Jeffrey W. Aubuchon

Heart-warming books from 92252 Press and available from online booksellers and independent retailers.

Put Your Toe In The Pacific
ISBN: 978-1734059267

Father Michael H. Custer, O.S.B. (1910-2006) lived as a monk of Saint Anselm Abbey for more than seventy years. In that time, he befriended thousands of students, families, and faculty members from Saint Anselm College. *Put Your Toe in the Pacific* is a collection of Father Michael's humorous wisdom as well as memories from an unlikely friendship at the end of his life.

Flight School: Lessons with Peter Pan
ISBN: 978-1734059229

When high school students in rural Massachusetts staged "Peter Pan" as their annual musical, they looked to soar just like Mary Martin. *Flight School* tells the inspiring journey of this community brought together by a century-old story and the financial, technical, and social challenges these students overcame in their voyage to Neverland. You'll believe you can fly with them!

Made in United States
North Haven, CT
28 November 2024

60484104R00068